THE

good

PORTION

The Good Portion

Heidi Baird

Hope in Truth Ministry
© 2019 Heidi Baird

The names and details of some of the people and situations described in this book have been changed or presented in a composite form to ensure the privacy of those with whom the author has worked with.

ISBN-13: 978-1-7334872-0-7

Front and back cover, as well as all art work in this book were created by:

Suzanna Baird  @suzannabaird

Graphic Design — www.timothymershon.com

<u>Contact information for Heidi</u>

 @heidimbaird

@heidimbaird

hbaird@abiz4me.com

Dedication

To my Savior, Jesus Christ.

To my sweet husband for his steadfast, faithful and unconditional love toward me. Doing life by your side is priceless. You have been my biggest supporter throughout this project. If you had not stood by me there would be no book. Thank you... I love you dearly.

To all my kind and encouraging children and grandchildren, who patiently let me disappear to my bedroom for a month while I wrote out the passions of my heart in this book. You picked up the slack and gave me the freedom to focus and plug away day after day, long into the night. So grateful for each of you ... kisses and hugs from Mom/Nana!

Contents

Preface

What was to be a thirty-minute trip to the grocery store quickly turned into a two-hour ordeal. As I was walking to the checkout line, a lady stopped me to comment on how tall I was (I'm six feet tall). She was the sweetest woman and we struck up a conversation and soon, without warning, she began crying and sharing how rough her day had been. I think she just had to let it all out, and God graciously put me in her path. We walked over to the deli area where there were some tables. She continued to share her life's journey filled with such sadness.

My heart broke for precious Milly. She was carrying the load of the world on her shoulders and it was easy to see she had been doing so for many years. She was weighed down with a huge bag of hurts, shame, guilt, bitterness, anger, and so much fear. Years ago, Milly's burdensome bag was probably a bit smaller and a little lighter. The many hard years had continued to increase her load, filling it with great disappointments, deep regrets, and unmet expectations.

I had the great privilege of counseling Milly for the next year and a half. Every week she learned to see God with fresh, clean lenses. She really believed God could heal her brokenness: "He heals the brokenhearted and binds up their wounds" (Psalm 147:3). For the first time in her entire life, she realized that there was Someone who loved her unconditionally. He was gentle, patient, kind, and forgiving. Her heavy load became smaller and smaller as she learned to surrender to a Father she could trust. Soon, Milly found freedom from the bondage of bitterness, fear, and lies. God graciously gave Milly a new hope, joy, and peace she had never before experienced. Her radiant smile reflected a heart that was truly free to live in victory. Worshipping at the feet of her Savior became a sweet activity in Milly's life.

Nothing brings me greater joy than walking a woman to complete freedom in Christ, watching her worship with a surrendered heart, and seeing her delight in searching for treasures in God's Word. Nothing is more precious!

Over the years I have spent counseling women, I have been honored to have a front-row seat as I watch God take broken, angry, bitter women on a journey of surrender, healing, and victory. That front-row seat is a priceless, glorious seat that I am privileged to sit in week after week. Just the thought brings tears to my eyes, and I am truly humbled.

My sweet friend, I may not have the honor and privilege of sitting across from you right now, but as you read this book, let's pretend that I am. I wrote every word with you in mind. I thought of your brokenness, your rejection, your pain, your past, and the heavy load you carry all alone.

If you stick with me through the next ten weeks, we'll journey together through the pages of this book as you, step-by-step, allow God into those secret places, those deep, dark crevices of your heart that rarely see the light. You've carried the burden for so long, alone, exhausted, hopeless, all the while doing it with the best smile you could muster up. When you weren't secretly crying behind closed doors, you put on a good face and pretended for a while that things weren't that bad. Like He did for Milly, God promises you, "He heals the brokenhearted and binds up their wounds" (Psalm 147:3).

I can almost imagine us sitting together, week after week, me in my front-row seat watching God do a miraculous work in your life as He molds you into the beautiful woman He created and designed you to be. God defines you as His beloved, His chosen, and His treasure.

> I pray this for you as you journey through this book:
> For this reason, I kneel before the Father, from whom His whole family in heaven and on earth derives its name. I pray that out of His glorious riches He may strengthen you with power through His Spirit in your inner being, so that Christ may dwell in your Hearts through faith. And I pray that you, being rooted and established in love, may have power, together with all the saints, to grasp how wide and long and high and deep is the love of Christ, and to know this love that surpasses knowledge—that you may be filled to the measure of all the fullness of God. Now to Him who is able to do immeasurably more than all we ask or imagine, according to His power that is at work within us, to Him be glory in the church and in Christ Jesus throughout all generations, for ever and ever! Amen (Ephesians 3:14–21).

May God be glorified!
Heidi

Introduction - The Good Portion

The Good Portion is not your average book, so be warned. You will cry, just so you know what's coming. There will be some tears. Even my husband, who is not a crier, cried when he read portions of this book. The precious stories are filled with personal journeys of women just like you and me. You'll meet Cindy, Janice, Milly, Shelly, and others.

Along with these women, I will take you on my own personal journey through the struggles and trials that God has graciously walked me through. The story in chapter eight was one of the toughest stories for me to write. I never expected to have to say a final good-bye to my child. I share the moment we softly kissed and hugged our Matthew before God took him home. You will get an inside view of my journey from seasons of heartaches and brokenness to a life of glorious surrender, healing, and freedom. Through the transparency of my heart, I will give you a glimpse into my endearing, intimate walk and humble worship with my Father.

You will be inspired in Chapter 9 by a woman who had hit her wall. She was done with the madness and wanted to be set free from her crazy life. Her world had been wrecked by hurt and rejection, and this had led to a heart of bitterness, fear, and anger and a lot of sad choices. She felt trapped in a cycle of habitual sins she didn't know how to get out of. She felt lonely, devalued, and broken. She thought she would never truly break free from the prison she was in. You may feel like this woman, asking yourself, "Where is the hope in this craziness? How can I get out of the trap?"

The inspiration for this book, *The Good Portion*, actually comes from my many years of counseling women who were exhausted and could not take one more day of the facade. By the time these women were sitting in front of me, they were at their end. They had tried everything to find a way around the guilt, shame, and brokenness, in hopes of finding joy, contentment, and peace. Nothing had worked. In fact, they were falling further into despair and hopelessness. They yearned to have a sweet relationship with God, but something was hindering them. Their quiet times were flat and lifeless.

You, like these women, may want to stop believing the relentless lies that tell you to keep pushing forward, to stay busy, that there is no time for God. Daily lies come and you believe them. The busyness keeps you from ever challenging those lies. The cycle of habitual sins is wearisome. You try to make changes, but nothing works.

It may have been a while since you opened the pages of Scripture, but you may long to walk with your Father again and allow Him to unfold the treasures of His thoughts to you. He delights in you, He calls you His beloved, He defines you, and He chose you. God is holy, righteous and just, gentle, kind, forgiving, and merciful and welcomes you into sweet fellowship with Him. The only thing standing in the way is you. Stop running, being distracted, holding onto the bondage of sin and come sit at His feet and just worship. Come as you are. No need for a facade or fake smile. Tears are welcomed. Your Father offers sweet serenity, peace of mind, and tranquility of soul: "Come to me, all who labor and are heavy laden, and I will give you rest" (Matthew 11:28).

Chapter 1 in this book will start you on a journey with a woman who will change your heart forever. She figured out the answer to all the madness, craziness, and distractions we all face in this life. She also learned how to value the most important things necessary for true joy and contentment. She will encourage you to finish the book. She will cheer you on to not give up. By the end of Chapter 1, you will desperately desire what she has and you will want to do what is necessary to have that in your own life. This woman has no baggage, unforgiveness, bitterness, or anger in her heart. Yes, she is a sinner, just like you and me, but, she made an intentional choice to do what was right, no matter what. It's a beautiful story of a young girl who is an extraordinary example of what true worship looks like.

I literally cry every time I read Chapter 1 of this book. This precious scene is etched in my mind forever. Okay, just a heads-up, I cry through most of the heartwarming stories in this book. The sweet woman in the first chapter chose the one most necessary thing. This gal prioritized her relationships, she intentionally set aside time to reflect and ponder all that was good. She treasured time to be still and just listen … quietly listen. She did the one thing necessary, she chose the good portion … and it will never be taken away from her.

This keepsake journal is to be used as a companion with the book, *The Good Portion.*

Guide

How to use this book

✱ There are nine weeks of daily reading and intimate questions.

✱ I designed this book to be used as a group Bible study and in a personal manner during your intentional set-aside time with God.

✱   I encourage group accountability to keep you on track.

✱ You will need your Bible, the Companion Journal to write your answers in, as well as take notes, and a pen.

✱ Leave electronics behind. That way there are fewer distractions.

✱ My prayer is for you to be very intentional with this book and follow it through to the end.

✱ Seven of the chapters will cover a different root issue:

Identity - Lies - Fear - Idols - Bitterness - Anger - Bondage to Sin

✱ You will learn what these root issues are according to God's Word.

✱ You'll be led through a series of daily questions helping you determine if these are recurring habitual sins in your life.

✱ You will be given the opportunity to surrender, repent, ask for forgiveness, and be restored. You can find true freedom. This is the guide you will follow each day.

Chapters 1-9

Day 1

* Make sure to have your Bible, Companion Journal, and a pen.
* Pray before you start.
* Scripture Reading.
* Chapter Reading.
* Memory Verse.

Days 2 – 5

* Start in prayer. There is a guided prayer to help you.
* Scripture reading and meditation.
* Answer the questions.
* Worship and pray.

Day 6

The Good Portion - A Time of Worship

* This is the day of the week that you do as Mary did and sit for an extended amount of time in prayer and worship.

Chapter 10

Personal Sabbatical

This is a special opportunity for you to take a *Personal Sabbatical*. This will be a one-day commitment and will allow you to review the root issues once again and ask God to search your heart for any habitual sins to which you may be blinded. You may want to read through the guided suggestions and begin preparing your heart. Also, you will need to be intentional and set aside a date to make it happen.

30 Day Personal Devotional

This will encourage you to continue to walk with God in worshipping Him through the Word and Prayer.

1

One Necessary Thing

1 One Necessary Thing

Day 1

✳ Make sure to have your Bible, Companion Journal, and a pen.

✳ Pray before you start.

✳ Open your Bible and read the Scripture selected for today.

✳ Read Chapter 1 of The Good Portion.

✳ Begin learning your Scripture memory verse so you will be ready to recite it on Day 6.

Daily Scripture Reading - Luke 10:38-42

Scripture Memory - Psalm 96:8, 9

"*Ascribe to the Lord the glory due his name; bring an offering and come into his courts. Worship the Lord in the splendor of his holiness; tremble before him, all the earth.*"

Chapter 1

Two sisters, two distinct personalities, and two different motivations. One got it, one missed it. These two sisters are quite similar in some ways and so very different in others.

I always love a great story full of love, drama, relationships, and fancy dinner parties, and this particular story does not disappoint. Let's pretend you and I are invited to a beautiful dinner party as guests of Martha of Bethany, a town east of Jerusalem. The only problem is, as we wander the streets in this busy town, we realize we don't know where Martha lives. So we ask around. Everyone seems to be very familiar with Martha and her family, and they point us directly to her home with no problem.

Bethany is a community known for its acts of charity and kindness. Many homes are open to the poor and destitute. Martha is well known in Bethany and the surrounding villages for her excellent hospitality. She has a reputation as a woman who shows great kindness and sensitivity to the needs of others. She especially has a heart for the poor, sick, and rejected.

As we walk through the streets on our way to Martha's home, we hear rumors that Jesus will be passing through Bethany today. We hope to possibly get a glimpse of Him while we are visiting.

Soon we arrive at the home of Martha, her sister Mary, and her brother Lazarus. We are warmly greeted as we enter the house. We notice there is a sense of eager anticipation and excitement in the air. We ask someone what is going on. We are quickly informed that Martha has also invited Jesus to come dine at her home. "Now as they went on their way, Jesus entered a village. And a woman named Martha welcomed Him into her house" (Luke 10:38).

Wow! We have been invited to dine with Jesus this afternoon. This is going to be the dinner party of the year and we get to be a part of it.

A Hurried Pace

Let's learn a little more about our sweet host and her siblings. Some biblical historians believe that Martha was the older sister, which would give her the title of owner and head of the home. Martha lived in the house with her two siblings, Mary and Lazarus. They were a very close-knit family, and their love for one another was quite evident.

Martha was well known as a delightful host and showed great hospitality to all who knew her. She had a heart for the poor and opened her home to the needy. I imagine she took serious time, effort, and pleasure in cooking delectable dishes and setting a beautiful table to make all those who entered her home feel cared for. She truly had a servant's heart.

Martha and Mary had different roles at home due to their age and maturity. Martha, being the older sister, most likely managed the household and held a senior position to her siblings. We do not know how old they were, but, a few clues give us the impression that Mary and Lazarus might be younger than Martha. None of the three were married, which would have been unusual unless they were still youthful. The hurried pace of their lifestyle might indicate that they were still physically quite capable of hard work without becoming too tired. We also see that Jesus treated and spoke to Martha, Mary and Lazarus like an older, endearing brother might treat and speak to younger siblings. Back to our dinner party.

We hear a lot of commotion out on the front porch. Jesus has arrived. Everyone runs to greet Him, crowding around in hopes of being near Him. It is very clear that He is the honored guest this afternoon. Martha warmly hugs Jesus and welcomes Him in.

> He has such a sweet, tender relationship with them and speaks with kind warmth.

Observing Jesus's interactions with Martha, Mary, and Lazarus, leads me to believe they are all intimately close. He has such a sweet, tender relationship with them and speaks with kind warmth, care, and concern. "Now Jesus loved Martha and her sister and Lazarus" (John 11:5).

Martha enjoys hosting and showing hospitality to her guests, but Jesus is no ordinary guest. Martha decides to go above and beyond, making sure everything is just right. She decides that time is of the essence and wastes not one minute as she gathers all the needed supplies.

It is important that everything be in its proper place and arranged perfectly for their honored guest. Martha has a grand and wonderful dinner planned this afternoon. Her menu will include a healthy salad of mint, rue, coriander, green onions, thyme, chives, and lettuce. For the main dish, Martha plans to serve smoked fish with a hot mint sauce and mixed greens with lentils and beans. To top off this lovely afternoon, she will serve her guests dried apples sprinkled with toasted sesame seeds.

As we sit on the porch listening to Jesus teach, we can clearly see Martha rushing about in every direction throughout the house. She quickly grabs her finest table linens and neatly unfolds them, laying each cloth gently on the table, rubbing her hands across them to smooth out all the fold lines. She then dashes to the closet to collect her elegant stoneware dinner plates from the top storage shelf, wiping the dust off each dish. She handles them carefully and arranges each plate on the table in front of the individual cushions.

Martha takes great pride and feels it necessary to show her guests that she is the "hostess with the mostess." It is imperative that all of the preparations be absolutely perfect, not missing one detail. There isn't much time and there is still a list of things to do.

As we sit there listening to Jesus, we all encourage Martha to stop running around and come sit with us and hear Jesus share His thoughts about His ministry and the people He has encountered on all of his journeys. Martha is missing out. The meal can wait. An opportunity to hear the Words of Jesus is an incredible honor. We will help prepare for the meal after He is done, but we just can't leave in the middle. This is an opportunity we absolutely do not want to miss. We hang on His every word.

A nice warm breeze cools us as we sip on a nice cool drinks of water from the springs. Martha continues to race back and forth from the garden, to the kitchen, to the table, back and forth, scurrying past Jesus, making sure not to miss one important detail.

Unfortunately, she begins to realize that she doesn't have enough time to get everything done on her extensive list in a sufficient and orderly manner. She does not want to disappoint her guests by serving dinner late or worse, cold. It is becoming very clear that her grand plan and expectations to have everything just perfect are beginning to fall apart. Stressed and worried, she sees her well-executed plan unraveling.

As Martha is running to the kitchen to check on the side dishes, she stops in her tracks. She cannot believe her eyes. To her amazement, she sees her sister Mary just calmly and quietly sitting at Jesus's feet. "And she had a sister called Mary, who sat at the Lord's feet and listened to his teaching" (Luke 10:39). Martha is stunned. How could Mary be so thoughtless? Martha is sweating, panting, and already exhausted as she tries her best to be the perfect hostess for her welcomed guests.

"But Martha was distracted with much serving" (Luke 10:40).

Martha becomes frantic, she goes from frantic to panic, and she is clearly upset with her sister Mary. Not able to control her emotions and assuming that Jesus will undoubtedly come to her defense, she blurts out, "Lord, do you not care that my sister has left me to serve alone? Tell her then to help me" (Luke 10:40).

Martha feels it is completely unfair for her to tend to all the details of such an elaborate meal alone, as her sister just sits at Jesus's feet. Clearly, Mary is being very insensitive by ignoring Martha's need for help. Martha is greatly offended by Mary's uncaring attitude. With all the million details that still need to be accomplished, Martha cannot understand why Mary is choosing to disregard the work that so obviously needs to be done. Martha feels a great responsibility to entertain Jesus with the finest meal, but she cannot do it alone.

Okay, if we're gonna be totally and completely honest, we can all relate to Martha! How many of us have experienced that same scenario when we were hosting a dinner party? She was just trying to show great hospitality and be a sweet hostess for her very honored guest. I mean, it was Jesus, right? We would desire to put out our very best dishes and linen for such an amazing man as Jesus. It's easy to be sympathetic to her frustration.

Martha, Martha!

Martha was clearly upset. She was patiently waiting for Jesus to scold Mary and send her to help her sister. Martha was about at her end. Let's just say she was not a happy camper.

Jesus finally stops His teaching, turns to look at Martha, and in a kind tone says, "Martha, Martha, you are anxious and troubled about many things" (Luke 10:41). As we all sit there in complete silence, we are amazed to hear Jesus speak in such a tender, calm voice as He says her name, "Martha, Martha." It is obvious, by His tone, that He cares for her deeply and understands that her intentions are well-meaning. He is obviously aware that she is trying to do a good job as a hostess. She is putting a lot of energy, time, and thought into every detail. He understands that.

But what does Jesus do? He speaks to her heart. He points out that Martha's heart is anxious and troubled. Can't you just see Jesus sitting there teaching everyone, sharing His thoughts, as sweet Mary sits quietly at His feet, listening with great attention to His every word? But as He teaches, He also has an eye on Martha. He sees right through the fuss and bother, the hustle and bustle, and knows exactly what Martha is doing.

Have you been invited to someone's house for dinner and you arrive at their home only to find them working frantically in the kitchen, sweating, hurried, distracted, and anxious over all the details? You just sit there completely ignored by your hosts and you feel a little awkward, wishing that they wouldn't fuss over impressing you with this meal. You would rather they come and sit with you and relax. You came to spend time with the hosts. The meal is secondary to the whole evening.

Jesus sees the situation and He wants Martha to settle down, take a deep breath, stop running around, and come sit with Him. He would rather the meal be delayed and have Martha come sit with her sister Mary.

Anxious and Troubled

In Martha's desire to make everything perfect for Jesus's visit, she actually makes the atmosphere a stress-filled, anxious, troubled one. Jesus tenderly points out the truth to Martha by saying, "Martha, Martha, you are anxious and troubled about many things" (Luke 10:41). Martha was concerned about the temporary food while Mary valued the eternal, the Bread of Heaven, Jesus.

You will notice in this passage, that at no time, in any verse, does Jesus speak about the meal, all the preparations, or Martha's creative hosting skills or talented cooking abilities. No! He speaks to her about the most important issue, her heart. Let's look at this verse again, "Martha, Martha, you are anxious and troubled about many things" (Luke 10:41). Jesus kindly states the facts about Martha's heart issues. She is anxious and troubled. Martha is focused on physical issues.

She is looking at the material, physical labor of trying to please those around her, hoping to be noticed for her beautifully set table, delicious meal, and honored guests.

> Jesus tends to focus on our spiritual issues, the intentions of our heart, and the truth of our motives.

Don't you find it interesting that Jesus tends to focus on our spiritual issues, the intentions of our heart, and the truth of our motives? But, we tend to look at all the physical and emotional problems that so easily distract us.

Verse 40 tells us that, "Martha was distracted with much service." This suggests that Martha was busily distracted with all the unnecessary, elaborate details. All of Martha's busyness and distractions were coming from a prideful heart. When we allow our prideful hearts to guide us, we will be led away by our emotions and will display wrong attitudes and actions.

What was Martha distracted from? Well, verse 42 answers that question. "But one thing is necessary. Mary has chosen the good portion, which will not be taken away from her" (Luke 10:42).

Who Do You Relate To?

One, just one, thing was necessary, and Martha was missing it. She felt like all of the fussing over elaborate details and hurriedly running about were what was necessary. She was missing the one necessary detail. Jesus!

Martha - Distracted, running about, fussing over the wrong details
Martha - Valued the temporal
Martha - Anxious and troubled

Mary - Quietly sitting still
Mary - Valued the eternal
Mary - Peaceful and joyful

The ONE thing necessary for all of us...
Value the eternal . . . WORSHIP, MEDITATE, AND LISTEN!

What is distracting you from making time to sit with Jesus? I'm not talking about the hurried day where we squeeze Jesus in. Maybe, we throw up a prayer at the stoplight on our way to the store or read a quick verse on our phone while waiting at the bank or sing along with praise songs on the radio as we sit in the drive-through. These are great additions to our day, but I'm talking about intentionally setting aside time to sit quietly before Him with nothing else distracting us.

> Nothing makes God more supreme and more central in worship than when people are utterly persuaded that nothing - not money or prestige or leisure or family or job or health or sports or friends - nothing is going to bring satisfaction to their sinful, guilty, aching hearts besides God.[1]

Come and sit with Him. Value Him! Value your relationship with Him like Mary did. He loves and values you. He wants you to value His truth, His thoughts, and the things He values. He wants to set you free from the lies and the distractions that so easily pull us from the one thing necessary, the most important thing in our lives, time with Him!

"But one thing is necessary. Mary has chosen the good portion, which will not be taken away from her" (Luke 10:42).

You must CHOOSE the one thing that is necessary, the good portion.

Reflection:

✦ Stop and pray right now and ask God to graciously and kindly reveal what you are really valuing above Him.

✦ Write a list of excuses that you use to not have time for God.

✦ Anything that you make more important than God is an idol. One by one, acknowledge what you make an idol (anything that keeps you from making time for God). Humbly confess these to God. Then ask for His gracious forgiveness for each one. Humbly ask God to forgive you for choosing to worship another god. I John 1: 9 tells us He promises to forgive us immediately when we ask.

✦ You can be free from the bondage of these idols right now through the power of God in Christ Jesus. Freedom in Christ is graciously offered to you this very moment. Who will you choose to worship?

✦ Ask God to give you the strength, discipline, and clarity to stay focused and see this book through to the end.

✦ Ask Him to help you learn to value Him above all else.

✦ Graciously allow Him to search out the areas of sin in your heart that you may be blinded to, and be willing to surrender them to Him as you go through this book.

✦ Thank Him for the opportunity to cleanse your heart of sin and walk in newness and freedom in Christ.

Day 2 - Worship the Splendor of His Holiness

* Make sure to have your Bible, Companion Journal, and a pen.
* Pray before you start. Use the guided prayer.
* Open your Bible and read the Scripture selected for today.
* Begin learning your Scripture memory verse and review it throughout the week.

Prayer: Use this prayer as a guide.

> *Dear God, my Precious Father, I come to this sweet time of worship, humbly sitting at Your feet. You are Holy, Holy, Holy, the Lord God Almighty. You are just, righteous, and pure. Thank You for giving me Jesus, my Savior. It is through the power of His mighty name that I come to You. Thank You for allowing me the privilege to sit in Your presence. Thank You for welcoming me into Your throne room. I surrender this sweet time of uninterrupted worship. May I feel Your kind presence, Your gentle nudge, and Your powerful wisdom. I pray that Your Word would give me insight, wisdom, and encouragement today. I praise You and thank You, Father. In Jesus's name, Amen.*

Recite your Scripture Memory - Psalm 96:8, 9.

"Ascribe to the Lord the glory due his name; bring an offering and come into his courts. Worship the Lord in the splendor of his holiness; tremble before him, all the earth."

Open your Bible to Psalm 96. Read the entire chapter once.

Day 2 Questions - Use your Companion Journal to answer the questions.

1. Pause and reflect on each verse. Pray them, one by one, back to God and humbly ask Him to help make each truth real in your life.

2. What does the word "worship" mean to you?

3. What does the phrase "God is Holy" mean to you?

4. What is the importance of surrendering set-apart time to be still before the Lord?

5. In Luke 10: 42, what does it mean that, "Mary has chosen the good portion and it will not be taken away from her."

Meditate on Psalm 96:1 – 3.

"Oh sing to the Lord a new song, sing to the Lord, all the earth! Sing to the Lord, bless his name; tell of his salvation from day to day. Declare his glory among the nations, His marvelous works among all the peoples!"

Close this time in grateful worship and prayer.

Day 3 - Worship the Splendor of His Majesty

* Make sure to have your Bible, Companion Journal, and a pen.
* Pray before you start. Use the guided prayer.
* Open your Bible and read the Scripture selected for today.
* Begin learning your Scripture memory verse and review it throughout the week.

Prayer: Use this prayer as a guide.

> *Dear Father, I humbly come before You, as David did, worshipping the splendor of Your Glory. I have such gratitude in my heart for this sweet time of worship You allow me to enjoy. May this set-apart time with You right now be glorifying in Your presence. I want to know the splendor of Your Glory like never before. I surrender my heart, mind, and thoughts to You. In the precious name of Jesus, I pray, Amen.*

Scripture Memory - Psalm 96:8, 9

"Ascribe to the Lord the glory due his name; bring an offering and come into his courts. Worship the Lord in the splendor of his holiness; tremble before him, all the earth."

Open your Bible to Psalm 96. Read the entire chapter once.

Day 3 Questions - Use your Companion Journal to answer the questions.

1. What do these words mean to you: "For great is the Lord, and greatly to be praised; He is to be feared above all gods" (Psalm 96: 4)?

2. In Psalm 96: 4, the word "gods" refers to any idol we choose to put above God. David said, "He is to be feared above all other gods." List the things you allow to get in the way of your surrendered time to sit still before Him each day.

3. How much intentional time each day do you set aside to sit quietly, without distractions, before God? Why do you choose that much time?

4. How would you describe the value Mary places on her relationship with Jesus (see Luke 10: 39; John 12: 3)?

Meditate on Psalm 96:4 – 6.

"For great is the Lord, and greatly to be praised; he is to be feared above all gods. For all the gods of the peoples are worthless idols, but the Lord made the heavens, Splendor, and majesty are before him; strength and beauty are in his sanctuary."

Close this time in grateful worship and prayer.

Day 4 - Worship the Splendor of His Glory

* Make sure to have your Bible, Companion Journal, and pen.

* Pray before you start. Use the guided prayer.

* Open your Bible and read the Scripture selected for today.

* Begin learning your Scripture memory verse and review it throughout the week.

Prayer: Use this prayer as a guide.

> *Dear Father, You are worthy of all my praise and adoration. I humbly come before You with a surrendered heart. I choose to set aside all other distractions and wholly worship You. Nothing is worth more than Your Holiness. Father, help me to see You in all Your majesty, strength, and beauty today. I am grateful that You give me set-aside time to be still and hear Your words. I desire You above all others. I surrender this time to You. In Jesus's holy name, Amen.*

Scripture Memory - Psalm 96:8, 9

"Ascribe to the Lord the glory due his name; bring an offering and come into his courts. Worship the Lord in the splendor of his holiness; tremble before him, all the earth."

Open your Bible to Psalm 96. Read the entire chapter once.

Day 4 Questions - Use your Companion Journal to answer the questions.

1. Read Psalm 96: 7, 8 and describe what you think the word "ascribe" means.

2. What are we to "ascribe" to?

3. Why does David find God's glory so important, and how many times does he mention it in Psalm 96?

4. Describe your view of God's glory.

Meditate on Psalm 96:7 – 10.

"Ascribe to the Lord, O families of the peoples, ascribe to the Lord glory and strength! Ascribe to the Lord the glory due his name; bring an offering, and come into his courts! Worship the Lord in the splendor of holiness; tremble before him, all the earth! Say among the nations, 'The Lord reigns! Yes, the world is established; it shall never be moved; he will judge the peoples with equity.'"

Close this time in grateful worship and prayer.

Day 5 - Worship the Splendor of His Faithfulness

* Make sure to have your Bible, Companion Journal, and pen.

* Pray before you start. Use the guided prayer.

* Open your Bible and read the Scripture selected for today.

* Begin learning your Scripture memory verse and review it throughout the week.

Prayer: Use this prayer as a guide.

> *Dear God, I praise You for choosing me, delighting in me and calling me Your child. I am humbled to sit before You. The splendor of Your righteousness is beautiful. Knowing that You are righteous, steadfast, and unmovable brings me great comfort and security. I praise You and give You all the glory due Your name. It is in the mighty name of Jesus, I pray, Amen.*

Scripture Memory - Psalm 96:8, 9

"Ascribe to the Lord the glory due his name; bring an offering and come into his courts. Worship the Lord in the splendor of his holiness; tremble before him, all the earth."

Open your Bible to Psalm 96. Read the entire chapter once.

Day 5 Questions - Use your Companion Journal to answer the questions.

1. David's descriptive words in Psalm 96: 11–13 are beautiful. He uses words like "be glad," "rejoice," "roar," "exult," and "sing for joy." All of creation worships the Creator. Describe how you can reflect some of these words to worship God today:

Be Glad-

Rejoice-

Exult (or Proclaim)-

Sing for Joy-

2. David says, in Psalm 96: 13, that God will judge the world in righteousness and His people in faithfulness. What does that mean?

3. List specific ways you see God's faithfulness in your life.

4. Use your list, from #3, to pray and thank God for His faithfulness in your life. Stop and do that right now.

Meditate on Psalm 96:11 – 13.

"Let the heavens be glad, and let the earth rejoice; let the sea roar, and all that fills it; let the field exult, and everything in it! Then shall all the trees of the forest sing for joy, before the Lord, for he comes, for he comes to judge the earth. He will judge the world in righteousness, and the peoples in his faithfulness."

Close this time in grateful worship and prayer.

Day 6 - The Good Portion - A Time of Worship

This is the day of the week that you do as Mary did and sit for an extended amount of time in prayer and worship. Block out at least an hour, perhaps more, once a week, to have extended time to be still, sit quietly all by yourself, and simply worship your Father.

Use Psalm 96 to guide your praise for God.

1. Praise (Use Psalm 96 to guide you).

2. Gratitude (Use Psalm 96 to guide you).

3. Worship (Sing).

4. Cry out to God with your joys, hurts, sadness, pain, guilt, shame, and repentance.

5. Close your prayer time by quoting a few verses from Psalm 96 that you have memorized and saying them to God. Hiding God's Word in your heart is a beautiful way to show God that you value Him and His thoughts. The goal is to crowd out our faulty thinking and replace our thoughts with His truth.

6. Read the Scriptures below twice through. The first time, substitute Martha's name for yours, and the second time you read through it, substitute Mary's name for yours.

"And she had a sister called Mary, _____ who sat at the Lord's feet and listened to his teaching. But Martha_____ was distracted with much serving. And she went up to him and said, "Lord, do you not care that my sister has left me to serve alone? Tell her then to help me." But the Lord answered her, "Martha, Martha,_____, _____ you are anxious

and troubled about many things, but one thing is necessary, Mary_____
has chosen the good portion, which will not be taken away from her" (Luke 10: 41-42).
The good portion is the eternal things we invest in that can never be taken away. May
Christ say of you.... but one thing is necessary, _____ has chosen the good
portion, which will not be taken away from her."

7. Pray and ask God to help you value eternal things and give you a heart
of worship like Mary's.

2

Identity

2 Identity

Chapter 2 - Identity

Day 1

* Make sure to have your Bible, Companion Journal, and pen.
* Pray before you start.
* Open your Bible and read the Scripture selected for today.
* Read Chapter 2 of The Good Portion.
* Begin learning your Scripture memory verse so you will be ready to recite it on Day 6.

Daily Scripture Reading - Psalm 139

Scripture Memory - Psalm 139:4 – 6

"Even before a word is on my tongue, behold, O Lord, you know it altogether. You hem me in, behind and before, and lay your hand upon me. Such knowledge is too wonderful for me; it is high; I cannot attain it."

Chapter 2

Just a few years into our marriage, I was cleaning our home and noticed that something was snagging my wedding ring. As I tried to untangle some thread that had neatly wrapped itself around my ring, I notice to my horror that the diamond in my ring had fallen out.

I carefully laid out a dark-colored linen cloth across the table and began to try to locate the diamond. I placed the knotted ball of thread on the linen and gently began to detangle each thread strand by strand, assuming my diamond must be caught up in the mess.

My Lost Diamond

After painstakingly separating each tiny thread, I noticed, well, nothing. Absolutely nothing! No diamond! Sadly, just a bunch of strings lay before me.

I got on my knees and prayed. I asked the Lord, in His kindness, if He would allow my eyes to find that precious little jewel. As long as I was on my knees, I thought, I might as well scavenge the floor for my treasured, glittery diamond. Inch by inch, I methodically scanned the floor for my precious, white gem, but to no avail.

> ... if He would allow my eyes to find that precious little jewel.

I ran to the vacuum cleaner, as I was sure it must have been sucked up while I was cleaning. I carefully removed the vacuum bag, took it outside on the back porch, laid a plastic tarp down and began sifting through the dust, dirt, legos, paper clips, toothpicks, hair, more thread and other things I could not identify. After thirty long minutes of separating the mess, I found.... NOTHING!

I began to pray again, asking God to graciously help me find my diamond on this unexpected treasure hunt. I so desperately wanted to find that diamond. I searched high and low. I tore the house apart from top to bottom, sideways, and inside out. Nothing, nothing, nothing!

I began to cry. I dreaded the thought that my precious keepsake diamond that my sweet husband had given me was lost forever. It was such a huge disappointment, and it broke my heart that day. After I informed my husband, he kindly let me know that the diamond was replaceable but I was not. He showed me his love and let me know just how valuable I was to him. What a gift.

I wondered for weeks why God allowed me to lose my diamond. He knew how special that diamond was to me. Why wouldn't He let me find it? I couldn't replace such a sentimental token of our marriage. Sure, it was just a ring, a diamond, a materialistic item, but, I had treasured it all the same.

I spent days continually looking for my diamond. I was obsessed with finding it. I couldn't just sit and rest in my own house without thinking about that gem. I found myself constantly digging in every corner, drawer, nook, and cranny throughout the day. But, as time went on, I began to look less and less. I knew the diamond was gone and never to be found again. I was sad, but time took away my tears.

A Token of Love

Years passed and one cool, sunny morning, I was sitting quietly before the Lord, praising, praying, and enjoying Psalm 139, when I felt the Lord take hold of my heart through the pages of Scripture. He showed me something that blew my mind.

He brought that diamond back to my thoughts. He showed me through His tender mercies one of the sweetest, most gracious truths in all of the Scriptures. That morning, God reminded me of something very intimately special about my relationship with Him. God used my lost diamond to teach me something very precious.

The value I placed on my lost diamond was more than just its actual monetary worth. I valued it because my loving husband gave it to me. The diamond was a token, a reminder of the covenant he made on our wedding day.

My husband expressed how much he valued me the day he put that ring on my finger and declared his covenant vows before God. That covenant, or promise, showed me the value my husband placed on God, on me, and on our marriage.

As I continued to read through Psalm 139, which I had read many times before, it seemed to take on a whole new importance to me. It literally took my breath away. Sitting there on the floor in my closet, the usual place where I have my quiet time with God, I was weeping as He brought my mind back to another incredible day in my life, years before.

Confused and Scared

It was the year 1975. God reminded me what a lost soul this sixteen-year-old high school girl was all those many years ago. I had no hope of where I'd spend eternity. The fear of death gripped me at night. I searched for answers, but to no avail. I wanted to know what I had to do to make it into heaven after I died. I was very scared of what would happen to me.

I was such a confused teen. Of course, I had friends, was outgoing, played sports and was highly involved in all of the usual school activities, but somehow I still felt so emotionally alone. I longed for someone to care for my thoughts, emotions, and, fears, not just the facade of this fun party girl. I bought the lie that my value was defined by what people thought of me. I desired and longed for so much more.

One beautiful day in 1975, God graciously provided an answer to my questions about eternity. He allowed me to sit down with my friend, Jan, who had recently become a Christian. On that amazing day in 1975, God used this sweet friend to share the truth about myself, God, and eternity. She showed me, through Scripture, that I was lost and on my way to hell because my sin separated me from a holy, just, righteous God (see Romans 3:23). That was a terrifying thought, as it should have been.

God is perfect, and to be reconciled to Him, there must be a perfect sacrifice for sin. So, in God's great mercy and love, (see John 3:16), He gave His only Son, Jesus, perfect and sinless, to become our sin sacrifice.

Jan guided me to a decision that day to accept Jesus Christ as my Savior, my only hope for reconciliation to God. The sin I deserved to pay for in hell was paid for, in full, by Jesus, for me and for all of mankind. I accepted the free gift of salvation for myself that very day. I was a new creation, an adopted child of God, an heir to the throne of God. I was His child forever. These verses became true of me that day:

"But when the fullness of time had come, God sent forth his Son, born of woman, born under the law, to redeem those who were under the law, so that we might receive adoption as sons" (Galatians 4:4–5).

"But to all who did receive Him, who believed in His name, He gave the right to become children of God" (John1:12).

Now, back in my closet, I was reminded of that incredible moment, the moment I was brought into the family of God, I just wept. Not only was I crying over that day back in 1975, but I was also crying this day because of who God was and how much He loved me. How grateful, privileged, and in awe I was to be called His child and to have such an intimate relationship with the God of the universe, the almighty King, the Eternal One, the Alpha and the Omega, the I AM, and my loving heavenly Father.

He calls me into fellowship with Him and desires to have an intimate relationship with me. He says I am valuable to Him and He treasures me. He treasures me far above the value I placed on my lost diamond. And that's when it hit me. I valued my diamond because it was a token of a covenant. That day in my closet, through my tears, I realized that God had made a covenant with me as well, and Jesus is the beautiful token God used to make His covenant with me.

> He says I am valuable to Him and He treasures me.

Jesus is the brilliant Jewel of the Universe. The One we all look to as the magnificent reflection of the glory of God. The One who we look to as the

Promised Savior, His living covenant with us.

I thought again about the diamond that I had lost. It was beautiful and had great value to me because of what the ring represented, a covenant and a promise. But God gave me something more astounding, more breathtaking, and more stunning. The most beautiful token I could ever imagine. He gave me Jesus. He is the most valuable token God could have ever given me in all of eternity. He sacrificed His only Son to make a covenant with me. Just like I had to accept the ring on my wedding day, I had to accept the gift of Jesus that God was offering me. Knowing that God will never break His covenant because of the finished work of Jesus on the cross, I am His forever.

God-Pleasers or People-Pleasers?

Why all the tears that day in my closet? Because I realized that God places a great value on my relationship with Him. He treasures me, He desires me, He delights in me, and He cares about my thoughts, my hurts, and my heart.

Tears of immense gratitude flowed! Oh, how intimate and loving is my Father! I am in awe of Him! I am so grateful to be His child, forever. Turn to Psalm 139.

"O Lord, you have searched me and known me! You know when I sit down and when I rise up; you discern my thoughts from afar. You search out my path and my lying down and are acquainted with all my ways. Even before a word is on my tongue, behold, O Lord, you know it altogether. You hem me in, behind and before, and lay your hand upon me. Such knowledge is too wonderful for me; it is high; I cannot attain it" (Psalm 139:1–6).

Sometimes when I feel sad, hurt, misunderstood, frustrated, fearful, or worried, and I feel like no one understands me or cares for my concerns, I'll open my Bible and read David's beautiful prayer in Psalm 139. This helps me to take my eyes off the lies and remember the truth of who I am in Christ. How valued I am by my Father through Jesus.

Diamonds are valuable, and one of the most precious gems in creation. They are rare, beautiful, and highly prized. But they are nothing compared to the value God places on us because of His Son.

Do we value what God thinks about us? Do we care what others think about us? Most of us, if we're honest, would say we struggle with being "people pleasers" more than "God pleasers." We put a lot of thought into what we might say or do to impress others, painting a picture of ourselves that will garnish us with the most accolades, give us the most reassurance, and boost our pride. Fear of man is a trap we are capable of in our flesh.

"The fear of man lays a snare, but whoever trusts in the Lord is safe" (Proverbs 29:25). Many times we take our past hurts, guilt, shame, and pain, put them in the equation of our decision making, and decide:

✦ I was hurt when I was young + I'll get hurt again = Retreat
✦ I failed when I tried that + I can never accomplish it = Give up
✦ I can't get into a relationship + it will fail again = Stay single
✦ I stumble over my words + I'll make a fool of myself = Speak less
✦ I have guilt over past sin + I will be rejected if they find out = Keep it a secret
✦ I was lied to + It will happen again = Trust no one
✦ I was never loved + I'll never be loved = Worthless

Past issues + lies = self-protection

Can you see how we protect and value ourselves in a very destructive way? Many of our unhealthy conclusions lead us to a life of fear, worry, bitterness, anger, and self-destructive behaviors. We emotionally put up so many walls to try and keep out the truth of the root issues of our hearts.

Whom Do Your Fear?

In *When People are Big and God is Small,* Ed Welch makes a good point, "When God and spirituality are reduced to our standards or our feelings, God will never be to us the awesome Holy One of Israel. With God reduced in our eyes, a fear of people will thrive." [2]

Whom do you fear? Whom have you given the power to define you? Whoever you feel the greatest need to impress is the person you have given the power to define you.

God knows we are sinful. That's why Christ died. We needn't act like we have it all together. God values us through His Son. He redeemed us and is molding us into the image of His Son. "But God shows His love for us in that while we were still sinners, Christ died for us" (Romans 5:8). That is the ultimate value God places on us.

God created you and did so with great intentionality and purpose. David understood that. Do you? Do you desire to know God's thoughts? Do you care what concerns God? In Psalm 139:7–8, David says that God's thoughts are precious to him: "How precious to me are your thoughts, O God! How vast is the sum of them! If I would count them, they are more than the sand. I awake, and I am still with you."

God used my diamond to remind me of my great worth to Him. My prayer for you, like the apostle Paul, is for you to know the incredible depth of God's love for you.

> "For this reason I bow my knees before the Father, from whom every family in heaven and on earth is named, that according to the riches of his glory he may grant you to be strengthened with power through his Spirit in your inner being, so that Christ may dwell in your hearts through faith—that you, being rooted and grounded in love, may have strength to comprehend with all the saints what is the breadth and length and height and depth, and to know the love of Christ that surpasses knowledge, that you may be filled with all the fullness of God. Now to him who is able to do far more abundantly than all that we ask or think, according to the power at work within us, to him be glory in the church and in Christ Jesus throughout all generations, forever and ever. Amen" (Ephesians 3:14–21).

Reflection:

✦ Stop and pray right now and ask God to graciously and kindly reveal the lies you believe about your identity in Christ. Read through the chart at the end of this chapter.

✦ Write a list of who you are in Christ. Why is it hard or not so hard to believe these truths?

✦ Read Psalm 139: 1-6 in your Bible and describe how that makes you feel.

✦ You can be free from the bondage of the lies you have believed about who you are in Christ. Right now through the power of God in Christ Jesus, ask Him to forgive you for believing the enemy's lies over His truth. Freedom in Christ is graciously offered to you this very moment. Whom will you choose to worship?

✦ Close in a time of worship, reading through Psalm 139 once again.

Day 2 - Identity

* Make sure to have your Bible, Companion Journal, and pen.

* Pray before you start. Use the guided prayer.

* Open your Bible and read the Scripture selected for today.

* Begin learning your Scripture memory verse and review it throughout the week.

Prayer: Use this prayer as a guide.

> *Dear Gracious Father, I know my heart wanders from You and I am prone to listen to the lies of the enemy. I need Your strength and power to overcome my sinful thoughts. Thank You for choosing me and saving me through Jesus. I ask You to please open my eyes to the lies I believe and help me see Your truth and obey it. In Jesus's merciful name, Amen.*

Recite Your Scripture Memory - Psalm 139:4 – 6.

"Even before a word is on my tongue, behold, O Lord, you know it altogether. You hem me in, behind and before, and lay your hand upon me. Such knowledge is too wonderful for me; it is high; I cannot attain it."

Open your Bible to Psalm 139. Read the entire chapter once.

Day 2 Questions - Use your Companion Journal to answer the questions.

1. What does it mean to you to be valued by God?

2. In Psalm 139: 1-5, what does David say God knows about him?

3. What does it mean to you personally when you say, "O Lord, you have searched me and known me?"

4. If God were going to write out a description of you, what would He say?

Meditate on Psalm 139:1 – 3.

"O Lord, you have searched me and known me! You know when I sit down and when I rise up; you discern my thoughts from afar. You search out my path and my lying down and are acquainted with all my ways."

Close this time in grateful worship and prayer.

Day 3 - Identity

* Make sure to have your Bible, Companion Journal, and pen.

* Pray before you start. Use the guided prayer.

* Open your Bible and read the Scripture selected for today.

* Begin learning your Scripture memory verse and review it throughout the week.

Prayer: Use this prayer as a guide.

> *Dear Holy Father, You are Worthy because You are God. The I AM. The Mighty One. I ask You to help me to value the things You value, to love the things You love, and to be continually transformed into the image of Your Son Jesus, in whose name I pray, Amen.*

Recite Your Scripture Memory - Psalm 139:4 – 6.

"Even before a word is on my tongue, behold, O Lord, you know it altogether. You hem me in, behind and before, and lay your hand upon me. Such knowledge is too wonderful for me; it is high; I cannot attain it."

Open your Bible to Psalm 139. Read the entire chapter once.

Day 3 Questions - Use your Companion Journal to answer the questions.

1. According to Psalm 139: 1-2, how does David say his transgressions will be blotted out?

2. Why is it important to acknowledge that our sin is against God?

3. What past or present issues keep you from seeing yourself as valued?

4. What truths do you see in Psalm 139, verses 3 and 4, in light of your past and present issues?

Meditate on Psalm 139:4 – 6.

"Even before a word is on my tongue, behold, O Lord, you know it altogether. You hem me in, behind and before, and lay your hand upon me. Such knowledge is too wonderful for me; it is high; I cannot attain it. "

Close this time in grateful worship and prayer.

Day 4 - Identity

✱ Make sure to have your Bible, Companion Journal, and pen.

✱ Pray before you start. Use the guided prayer.

✱ Open your Bible and read the Scripture selected for today.

✱ Begin learning your Scripture memory verse and review it throughout the week.

Prayer: Use this prayer as a guide.

> *Dear Holy God, You alone are Holy. You have created all things in Your image, to reflect You and Your Son, Jesus Christ. I give You praise for Your Creative Hand in designing me so distinctly with great purpose. I love and praise You, in the glorious name of Jesus, Amen.*

Recite Your Scripture Memory - Psalm 139:4 – 6.

"Even before a word is on my tongue, behold, O Lord, you know it altogether. You hem me in, behind and before, and lay your hand upon me. Such knowledge is too wonderful for me; it is high; I cannot attain it."

Day 4 Questions - Use your Companion Journal to answer the questions.

1. What does it mean to you to know God protects you (Psalm 139: 5, 6)?

2. God says He values us because of His Son Jesus. Why is this important (see Romans 5: 8, Galatians 2: 20; John 1: 12)?

3. Do you ever feel like hiding from God? Why? How do you try to hide?

4. Even when we feel so far away from God, what does Psalm 139: 10 tell us?

Meditate on Psalm 139:9, 10.

"If I take the wings of the morning and dwell in the uttermost parts of the sea, even there your hand shall lead me, and your right hand shall hold me."

Close this time in grateful worship and prayer.

Day 5 - Identity

* Make sure to have your Bible, Companion Journal, and pen.
* Pray before you start. Use the guided prayer.
* Open your Bible and read the Scripture selected for today.
* Begin learning your Scripture memory verse and review it throughout the week.

Prayer: Use this prayer as a guide.

> *God, truly You are the Creator of all things. You are the God of the universe who put the stars in place and know their names. God, please help me to see You in all Your holiness, mercy, and grace. I need Your hand in my life to set me free from the lies I so easily believe. You call me Your child and You have chosen me. I need to feel Your perfect love in my life. Thank You for loving me. In the mighty name of Jesus, Amen.*

Open your Bible to Psalm 139. Read the entire chapter once.

Day 5 Questions - Use your Companion Journal to answer the questions.

1. In what ways did God know you before you were born (Psalm 139: 13-16)?

2. What are your thoughts about God knowing you so intimately?

3. List the ways you see David's hatred for sin and wickedness against God (see Psalm 139: 17-24). Describe how you should hate wickedness in your own heart.

4. David was very transparent with God in Psalm 139: 23, 24. In what ways do you find it is hard to be transparent with God?

Meditate on Psalm 139:23, 24.

"Search me, O God, and know my heart! Try me and know my thoughts! And see if there be any grievous way in me, and lead me in the way everlasting!"

Close this time in grateful worship and prayer.

Day 6 - The Good Portion - A Time of Worship

This is the day of the week that you do as Mary did and sit for an extended amount of time in prayer and worship. Block out at least an hour, perhaps more, once a week, to have extended time to be still, sit quietly all by yourself, and simply worship your Father.

1. Praise (Use Psalm 139 to guide you).

2. Gratitude (Use Psalm 139 to guide you in prayer).

3. Worship (Sing).

4. Pray
(ACTS - Adoration, Confession, Thanksgiving, and Supplication).

5. Thank God for His Word. Quote verses back to God that you memorized this week.

6. Confess the lies you choose to believe. Lies that God doesn't love you, wants to punish you, does not want to reconcile with you, does not care, does not value you through Jesus.

7. Write out a closing prayer committing to trust in God's love.

• I am a child of God. "But to all who have received him--those who believe in his name--he has given the right to become God's children" (John 1:12).	**• I am redeemed and forgiven by the grace of Christ** "In Him we have redemption through His blood, the forgiveness of our trespasses, according to the riches of His grace" (Ephesians 1:7).
• I am a branch of the true vine, and a conduit of Christ's life. "I am the true vine and my Father is the gardener. I am the vine; you are the branches. The one who remains in me--and I in him--bears much fruit, because apart from me you can accomplish nothing" (John 15:1, 5).	**• I have been sealed with the Holy Spirit of promise.** "And when you heard the word of truth (the gospel of your salvation)--when you believed in Christ--you were marked with the seal of the promised Holy Spirit" (Ephesians 1:13).
• I am a friend of Jesus. "I no longer call you slaves, because the slave does not understand what his master is doing. But I have called you friends, because I have revealed to you everything I heard from my Father" (John 15:15).	**• Because of God's mercy and love, I have been made alive with Christ.** "But God, being rich in mercy, because of his great love with which he loved us, even though we were dead in transgressions, made us alive together with Christ--by grace you are saved" (Ephesians 2:4-5).
• I have been justified and redeemed. "But they are justified freely by his grace through the redemption that is in Christ Jesus" (Romans 3:24).	**• I am a citizen of Heaven.** "But our citizenship is in heaven--and we also await a savior from there, the Lord Jesus Christ" (Philippians 3:20).
• My old self was crucified with Christ, and I am no longer a slave to sin. "But they are justified freely by his grace through the redemption that is in Christ Jesus" (Romans 3:24).	**• The peace of God guards my heart and mind.** "And the peace of God that surpasses all understanding will guard your hearts and minds in Christ Jesus" (Philippians 4:7).
• I will not be condemned by God. "For the law of the life-giving Spirit in Christ Jesus has set you free from the law of sin and death" (Romans 8:2).	**• I have been made complete in Christ.** "You have been filled in him, who is the head over every ruler and authority" (Colossians 2:10).
• As a child of God, I am a fellow heir with Christ. "And if children, then heirs (namely, heirs of God and also fellow heirs with Christ)--if indeed we suffer with him so we may also be glorified with him" (Romans 8:17).	**• God supplies all my needs.** "And my God will supply your every need according to his glorious riches in Christ Jesus" (Philippians 4:19).
• I have been accepted by Christ. "Receive one another, then, just as Christ also received you, to God's glory" (Romans 15:7).	**• I am God's workmanship created to produce good works.** "For we are his workmanship, having been created in Christ Jesus for good works that God prepared beforehand so we may walk in them" Ephesians 2:10.

3
Lies

3 Lies

Chapter 3 - Lies

Day 1

* Make sure to have your Bible, Companion Journal, and pen.
* Pray before you start.
* Open your Bible and read the Scripture selected for today.
* Read Chapter 3 of <u>The Good Portion</u>.
* Begin learning your Scripture memory verse so you will be ready to recite it on Day 6.

Daily Scripture Reading - Genesis 3

Scripture Memory - Hebrews 4:12

"For the Word of God is living and active, sharper than any two-edged sword, piercing to the division of soul and of spirit, of joints and of marrow, and discerning the thoughts and intentions of the heart."

Chapter 3

Do some of these words stir your heart right now?

Discouraged	Guilty	Deceived
Hopeless	Shameful	Fearful
Unworthy	Worried	Angry
Overwhelmed	Frustrated	Bitter
Defeated	Anxious	Critical

I believe most of us would say at least some of these are all too familiar to us. You are not alone. We all struggle with these thoughts and feelings at some point in our lives. They are common to all of us. As Solomon tells us in Ecclesiastes, there is nothing new under the sun.

I went through seasons where I struggled with some of these issues. Homeschooling eight children might have brought me a little frustration at times, even leaving me feeling overwhelmed. The death of one of our children left me feeling extremely discouraged and sad. Facing the news of cancerous melanoma drove me to anxiety, worry, and fear, and there were times I felt less than attractive after delivering my babies, which gave me a sense of shame as I looked in the mirror.

I am sure you have your own memories and seasons when you felt you could relate with these issues. Maybe you are dealing with some right now. You might feel like these issues are more prevalent in our culture today, due to our overly busy, distracted lives and all the comparing that happens on social media. We face so many pressures, concerns, and stresses just trying to keep up with everyone else.

I'd like to think that these emotional and physical stresses we struggle with are a modern-day problem, but, unfortunately, these problems have been around for thousands of years. Remember? There is nothing new under the sun.

Doubt and Lies

We only have a few characters in our story today, four to be exact. We have two people, one sneaky guy, and a Ruler, some animals, and lots of angels. Let me introduce you to our famous characters. There is God - mighty Creator of the universe, Satan - a shrewd and evil serpent, Adam - first human man, and Eve - first human woman. With our characters introduced, let's dive into our story and get a better glimpse of these folks, who, by the way, make some pretty big decisions that change the course of humanity forever.

The whole story takes place in one of the most beautiful, lusciously green and fruitful places on the earth, called the Garden of Eden. Temperatures were more than likely a comfortable 75° with warm sunny days. Fruit trees, nuts, and berries were huge and abundant. God, the Creator in the story, says He was very satisfied with all that He had made. Genesis 1:31 says, "God saw everything that He had made, and behold, it was very good."

Adam and Eve, an adorable couple, had the entire garden to themselves. A private paradise to explore and enjoy. They were living the good life. Now let's talk about this gal Eve. If she had social media in the garden, I'm sure she would have posted many pictures of her gorgeous, luxurious surroundings for all to enjoy. Wow! Talk about some amazing backdrops. We might think to ourselves, as we flipped through her amazing pics ...

"Now that girl has got it all. Perfect husband, perfect neighborhood, perfect company, and everything she wants is at her fingertips. She doesn't even sweat. She doesn't have to color her hair, shave her legs, worry about the latest fashion, be distracted by a busy calendar, or worry about a platform, social media, or the latest diet. She is totally living the good life."

That is quite a dreamy scene. We can only imagine such a life. But Eve's perfect, wonderful, safe world would soon change forever. So, how do we go from that beautiful scene with Eve in her perfect world to a scene where Eve is being kicked out of the neighborhood? She loses all her sumptuous, delightful surroundings, loses her perfect status and her perfect world. We find her on the run, hiding in shame and regret, wearing animal skins and living in utter fear. What in the world happened?

Turn in your Bible to Genesis 3 and begin reading in verse 1. Scene one - Enter nasty, evil, character. He shows up in verse 1: "Now the serpent was more crafty than any other beast of the field that the Lord God had made" (Genesis 3:1).

Our crafty, sneaky, king of all lies is in Eve's perfect world. How'd he get in there? Well, God allowed him in. We'll see why in a bit. Satan, a perfect angel at one time, rebelled against God and was cursed. He has come to wreak havoc in the garden and havoc he wreaks.

Satan is described as a murderer, a liar, and the father of all lies. The epitome of evil of all evils. He is actually known as the devil, which means slanderer, and satan, which means accuser. He certainly lives up to his names in a very huge, destructive way.

Now, Adam and Eve were enjoying a sweet day of fellowship with God in the garden. God, our true Super Hero of all Super Heroes, is the kind and compassionate character in this story. He is the Creator, the Protector, and the Redeemer. Adam and Eve were privileged to walk in the garden with God all day, enjoying sweet fellowship.

Satan was staked out in a tree in the garden, spying on Adam and Eve, and was patiently taking note of their happy, perfect little world. He saw all that went on between them and hated it.

One fateful day, Satan found Eve alone, with Adam off in the distance. He knew God had given Eve a husband for her protection, and Satan patiently waited until Adam was tending to other things. Eve was Satan's target, and he had a grand scheme to destroy her and Adam and all of their descendants forever.

He has come to wreak havoc in the garden and havoc he wreaks.

Eve, up to this point, had not experienced sin and evil. She was created with a free will and was capable of sin; she just had not faced evil yet. But, if Satan had his way, Eve would soon find out the devastating destruction of just one wrong choice.

There were many trees in the garden, but one specific tree God had strategically placed in the middle of the garden and named it the Tree of Knowledge of Good and Evil, with one important rule.

"And the LORD God commanded the man, 'You are free to eat from any tree in the garden; but you must not eat from the tree of the knowledge of good and evil, for when you eat of it you will surely die'" Genesis 2:16.

God put the tree there to allow Adam and Eve to prove their fidelity and loyalty by obeying Him. If they were not given a choice, they would have been robots, unable to have relationships or to choose to love. God had to allow Adam and Eve to be tempted by Satan and force them to make a choice, to obey God or disobey God, to believe God or doubt God.

Lie #1 - Doubt

Now, Eve wasn't even thinking about eating the fruit of that tree. She was content with her life. She trusted and believed in God, and her world was peaceful and good. But here came the evil crafty one. If you were going to trick someone who has everything and wants for nothing, you better be a pretty cleaver salesman.

Adam and Eve knew that God had commanded them not to eat the fruit from the special tree in the garden. If they did they would surely die. That tree was set aside for a purpose and God gave them a command along with a consequence if they disobeyed.

Let's be reminded of this verse again, because this is the key to the whole scene: "And the Lord God commanded the man, saying, 'You may surely eat of every tree of the garden, but of the tree of the knowledge of good and evil you shall not eat, for in the day that you eat of it you shall surely die'" (Genesis 2:16–17).

Satan knew what God had said. He knew Eve was also aware of what God had said. So his first trick was to entice Eve to doubt God. "He said to the woman, Did God actually say, 'You shall not eat of any tree in the garden'" (Genesis 3:1)?

Did you catch that? Satan asked her a question, "Did God ACTUALLY say?" Satan had two agendas here. He wanted to deceive Eve about God's character and God's Word. His first trick was planting a seed of doubt about the validity of God's Word and encouraging her to question God's intentions.

But, look at how Eve answered the serpent. "And the woman said to the serpent, "We may eat of the fruit of the trees in the garden, but God said, 'You shall not eat of the fruit of the tree that is in the midst of the garden, neither shall you touch it, lest you die'" (Genesis 3:2).

Now Eve did not quote God exactly here. He said, "You may surely eat of every tree of the garden, but of the tree of the knowledge of good and evil you shall not eat, for in the day that you eat of it you shall surely die" (Genesis 2:16–17).

Notice how Eve twisted that last phrase? She says, "lest you die" rather than "you shall surely die." She misquoted the absolute of God's Word and skewed the consequences a bit. That was a huge mistake. He said that they would absolutely die if they ate of the tree and she turned it just a bit and said there was a great possibility they might die. It's subtle, but indicative of the trickiness of our sinful reasoning.

Without God involved in my reasoning process, the doubts

Satan picked up on this misquote and zeroed in on it. He proceeded to deceive her to assure her of perfect impunity and convince her that she would surely not die. He planted doubt and a lie. Alone in her thoughts, Eve might be asking herself ...

"Did I really hear God correctly?"
"Did He really say that?"
"Did God really mean what He said?"
Doubt, doubt, doubt.

Have you ever doubted God and His word? I know I have. Oh, those deadly convos we have with ourselves sometimes. The truth is, me and myself should never have conversations. Without God involved in my reasoning process, the doubts will come and the results can be downright scary. Satan loves to jump in and throw out lies and some near truths, even quote God's words, putting his own spin on it to deceive me. If I'm not careful, me and myself will mull over those lies, debate the lies, and then try to fit the results into my very selfish agenda.

We can obviously see how Satan twisted God's words to Eve. The enemy knew Eve wouldn't believe him unless she doubted God's true intentions. Satan knew that death and separation were to be the punishment for their disobedience and he was determined to trick them into eating from the tree.

The biggest danger in this passage is that Satan got Eve to interact with him. He creatively encouraged her to converse with him. She should have walked away the minute Satan misquoted God, dismissed his deceit, and given him no opportunity to speak to her. Shut him off. Chose to believe God and trust His word. But she not only conversed with him, she also allowed the seed of doubt to be planted in her heart.

Lie # 2 - Temptation

Satan planted doubt with Lie # 1 and wasted no time as he strategically moved into Lie # 2. He enticed her into believing that she could have even more than she already had, which was a bit tricky for Satan, since Eve already had everything and was content. This tells me that no matter how much I have, even feeling completely satisfied, I can always be tempted to want more. Eve had it all and even she was enticed to want more. What chance do we have?

The lie of covetousness and envy was now introduced into Eve's doubting, curious, and confused mind. Eve had everything to make her the happiest woman on earth (literally, since she was the only woman on earth). She had everything … except … Satan whispered in her ear, "Sure, Eve, you have everything, EXCEPT …!"

Until that moment, Eve didn't even know what she was missing. But Satan carefully and creatively used all the right words to point out what she DIDN'T have. He didn't point to all that she DID have, no, he tempted her with the ONE thing she didn't have. What was that? Genesis 3: "… your eyes will be open to good and evil and you will be like God…" What was the one thing Satan led Eve to believe she didn't have? The ability to see good and evil like God. For the first time, she was tempted to know what good and evil were.

Satan came across as this neutral bystander, caring for Eve's well-being, and if she stuck with him, she would experience things at a whole new enlightened level. He convinced her that God was holding out on her. Satan presented himself as the fun guy who had the real inside scoop to all the secrets of the garden.

Satan cleverly painted a lie that would lead Eve to question God's original command and protection of them. She bought the lie and doubted God and His word. Sadly, Satan had her.

We are just like Eve many times. We are content in life until we observe someone else's life. We see another couple and wish for a nicer husband like that one, or children that obey, like those kids, or a house like hers. We are perfectly content with our lives until we see someone else's life. For example, when we visit someone's home that is clearly much larger than ours, is more beautifully decorated, and has all the modern appliances, our eyes are opened to what we don't have. We carefully look at everything in that home with great detail, wishing we had that gorgeous living room furniture, those elegant granite counter tops, or that beautiful antique Persian rug. We believe a lie that we are missing out and deserve more. The lie takes root and when we come home and look at our little house, we are deceived into thinking its inferior and we deserve more. We were perfectly content until our eyes lusted and we bought the lie.

God says that the only hope for us to be completely satisfied in this life is to keep our minds on Him in full trust. "You keep him in perfect peace whose mind is stayed on You, because he trusts in You" (Isaiah 26:3). This is our safeguard from the enemy's lies.

Lie # 3 - Consequences

Satan tricked Eve and she fell for all the lies. She took her eyes off the truth and doubted God, reinterpreted His intentions, lusted for more. She also convinced Adam that he should enjoy the fruit with her. He chose to believe the lie as well, was enticed, gave in, and ate of the fruit. How many times have we persuaded others to join us in our sin, somehow feeling like that will ease the guilt a bit? Another lie of the enemy.

"So when the woman saw that the tree was good for food, and that it was a delight to the eyes, and that the tree was to be desired to make one wise, she took of its fruit and ate, and she also gave some to her husband who was with her, and he ate" (Genesis 3:6).

Sadly, that is the moment that changed life on earth forever. It only took six verses for Satan to successfully secure victory. He is the great accuser and slanderer, and the father of all lies. Adam and Eve were the first of many victims.

> Satan's Lie:
> Plants doubt
> against God and
> His Word.

God said there would be consequences for Adam and Eve's disobedience and He kept His promise. "To the woman, he said, 'I will surely multiply your pain in childbearing; in pain, you shall bring forth children. Your desire shall be contrary to your husband, but he shall rule over you'" (Genesis 3:16).

This next part of the story always makes me cry. Up to this point, Eve only knew perfect holiness. She had never seen evil. Can you imagine Eve's horror as she was face-to-face with evil for the first time? To know at that moment her entire perfect world of joy, peace, serenity, safety, and contentment was gone. Her life would never be the same again. In that instant, she so desperately wanted to take it all back.

"He drove out the man, and at the east of the garden of Eden he placed the cherubim and a flaming sword that turned every way to guard the way to the tree of life" (Genesis 3:24). Their one choice to believe a lie and act on it would haunt them the rest of their lives.

Satan's Lie:
Plants doubt against God and His Word.
Reinterprets God's motives.
Tempts us to be selfish.
Twists God's consequences for us.

Eve fell for them all. Eve would now experience the harsh reality of the words we discussed at the beginning of this chapter. For the first time, Eve knew what it meant to feel guilt, shame, deceit, discouragement, anxiety, and so on. She believed a lie and paid the consequences.

But, there is good news. This story in the garden is actually one of grace. Everything God does for His children is seasoned with tender grace. The garden is a story of immense forgiveness and redemption. From Genesis to Revelation, the story of God's kind redemption through Jesus is a beautiful picture of His unconditional grace.

> Our Lord Jesus is ever giving, and does not for a solitary instant withdraw His hand…the rain of His grace is always dropping, the river of His bounty is ever-flowing, and the wellspring of His love is constantly overflowing. As the King can never die, so His grace can never fail.[3]

By God's infinite grace, He continues to call us into sweet fellowship with Him. God is still God, and our actions can never change that. Adam and Eve's sin did not change God's character. His love is always steadfast and faithful, no matter what. We must keep our hearts and minds stayed on Him and His Word. He is good and worthy of our worship.

Reflection:

✦ Stop and pray right now and ask God to graciously and kindly reveal the lies of your heart, the lies that you are believing over His truth.

✦ Write a list of the lies that come to mind. Lies about His character, His Word, His faithfulness.

✦ One by one, acknowledge the lies you have been believing. Confess these to God. Then ask for His gracious forgiveness for each lie. Humbly ask God to forgive you for choosing not to believe Him. I John 1: 9 tells us that He promises to forgive us immediately when we ask.

✦ You can be free from these lies right now through the power of God in Christ Jesus. Freedom in Christ is graciously offered to you this very moment.

✦ Write out a prayer right now and then pray it back to God.

Day 2 - Lies

* Make sure to have your Bible, Companion Journal, and pen.
* Pray before you start. Use the guided prayer.
* Open your Bible and read the Scripture reading for today.
* Begin learning your Scripture memory verse and review it throughout the week.

Prayer: Use this prayer as a guide.

> *Dearest precious Father, I come in the name of Jesus, my Savior. My heart is full of praise for Your unfailing love. You are gracious and good and worthy of all my praise. I bow humbly before You as Your child. I give You my whole self in full surrender to Your will. May I receive Your wisdom through Your Word. I pray this in the precious name of Jesus, Amen.*

Recite Your Scripture Memory - Hebrews 4:12.

"For the Word of God is living and active, sharper than any two-edged sword, piercing to the division of soul and of spirit, of joints and of marrow, and discerning the thoughts and intentions of the heart."

Open your Bible to Genesis 3. Read the entire chapter one time through.

Day 2 Questions - Use your Companion Journal to answer the questions.

1. Describe what you think the garden may have looked like (see Genesis 2: 5-10).

2. What was the relationship between God, Adam, and Eve (see Genesis 1: 27-31)?

3. Describe the peace, joy, and security Adam and Eve must have felt in their perfect world.

4. Do you think we can have that same peace, joy, and security as a child of God now? Why or why not (see Galatians 5: 22-25)?

Meditate on Galatians 5:22 – 24.

"But the fruit of the Spirit is love, joy, peace, patience, kindness, goodness, faithfulness, gentleness, self-control; against such things, there is no law. And those who belong to Christ Jesus have crucified the flesh with its passions and desires."

Close this time in grateful worship and prayer.

Day 3 - Lie # 1 - Doubting

* Make sure to have your Bible, Companion Journal, and pen.
* Pray before you start. Use the guided prayer.
* Open your Bible and read the Scripture selected for today.
* Begin learning your Scripture memory verse and review it throughout the week.

Prayer: Use this prayer as a guide.

> *Father God, You are holy, righteous, and good. You have proven Your love to the world through Your Son, Jesus Christ. Because of Jesus, I have the hope of heaven and standing before Him, face-to-face, one day soon. Thank You for the Holy Spirit that gives me comfort and peace. Thank You for Your word that gives me insight and wisdom. I praise You for all that You are. I pray all of this in the power of Jesus's name, Amen.*

Recite Your Scripture Memory - Hebrews 4:12.

"For the Word of God is living and active, sharper than any two-edged sword, piercing to the division of soul and of spirit, of joints and of marrow, and discerning the thoughts and intentions of the heart."

Open your Bible to Genesis 3. Read the entire chapter one time through.

Day 3 Questions - Use your Companion Journal to answer the questions.

1. Describe Satan in Genesis 3: 1, 2.

2. In Genesis 3: 1, who is the first person Satan communicates with and what does he say?

3. What tactic does Satan use against Eve?

4. Why is questioning the authority of God's Word so destructive for you?

Meditate on John 1:1 – 5.

"In the beginning was the Word, and the Word was with God, and the Word was God. He was in the beginning with God. All things were made through him, and without him was not any thing made that was made. In him was life, and the life was the light of men. The light shines in the darkness, and the darkness has not overcome it."

Close this time in grateful worship and prayer.

Day 4 - Lie # 2 - Temptation

* Make sure to have your Bible, Companion Journal, and pen.
* Pray before you start. Use the guided prayer.
* Open your Bible and read the Scripture selected for today.
* Begin learning your Scripture memory verse and review it throughout the week.

Prayer: Use this prayer as a guide.

> *Father, Creator, and God, I come to You as Your precious child. Thank You for creating me and giving me life. Thank You for giving me Your indisputable, flawless Word. I am grateful for Your faithfulness and unmovable character. Thank You for being the Alpha and the Omega, the Beginning and the End. I give You this precious time and sit in a worshipful attitude. I pray in the matchless name of Jesus, my Savior, Amen.*

Recite Your Scripture Memory - Hebrews 4:12.

"For the Word of God is living and active, sharper than any two-edged sword, piercing to the division of soul and of spirit, of joints and of marrow, and discerning the thoughts and intentions of the heart."

Open your Bible to Genesis 3. Read the entire chapter one time through.

Day 4 - Use your Companion Journal to answer the questions.

1. Satan deceives Eve in the first verse. What is Eve's response to Satan in Genesis 3: 2?

2. What happens when we doubt God's Word (see 2 Timothy 4: 3-5)?

3. Eve's first mistake was to talk with Satan. We should never entertain anything that encourages us to doubt God. Every word of man should be examined through the filter of the Bible. God's Word is the final authority. How might you be encouraging your mind to be distracted by lies? Consider social media, movies, books. List your weaknesses.

4. Write out a commitment to God and ask Him to give you strength and wisdom to be on your guard against the lies of the enemy.

Meditate on Hebrews 4:12.

"For the Word of God is living and active, sharper than any two-edged sword, piercing to the division of soul and of spirit, of joints and of marrow, and discerning the thoughts and intentions of the heart."

Close this time in grateful worship and prayer.

Day 5 - Lie # 3 - Consequences

* Make sure to have your Bible, Companion Journal, and pen.

* Pray before you start. Use the guided prayer.

* Open your Bible and read the Scripture selected for today.

* Begin learning your Scripture memory verse and review it throughout the week.

Prayer: Use this prayer as a guide.

> *Dear God, thank You for allowing me the privilege and honor to call You my Father. I am eternally grateful to You for sanctifying me and covering me in Jesus's righteousness. I am forever your child and can never lose my position in Christ. Your Word is the truth and is unshakable. It is the authority on which I stand. I love You and Praise You in the Name of Jesus, Amen.*

Recite Your Scripture Memory - Hebrews 4:12.

"For the Word of God is living and active, sharper than any two-edged sword, piercing to the division of soul and of spirit, of joints and of marrow, and discerning the thoughts and intentions of the heart."

Open your Bible to Genesis 3. Read the entire chapter one time through.

Day 5 - Use your Companion Journal to answer the questions.

1. What did **God** say was the consequence of eating the fruit of the Tree of Good and Evil (see Genesis 2: 17)?

2. What did **Satan** say was the consequence of eating the fruit of the Tree of Good and Evil (see Genesis 3: 4)?

3. God sets up boundaries for our good because He loves us. These boundaries are good and protective. They are not burdensome. How did Satan entice Eve to eat of the fruit and go outside of God's boundaries?

4. What good boundaries are you ignoring just to have temporal pleasure? Write these down and then confess them to God and ask His forgiveness.

5. What consequences did Adam and Eve experience after they disobeyed (see Genesis 3: 7-13)?

Meditate on 2 Timothy 3:16

"All Scripture is breathed out by God and profitable for teaching, for reproof, for correction, and for training in righteousness."

Close this time in grateful worship and prayer.

Day 6 - The Good Portion - A Time of Worship

This is the day of the week that you do as Mary did and sit for an extended amount of time in prayer and worship. Block out at least an hour, perhaps more, once a week, to have extended time to be still, sit quietly all by yourself, and simply worship your Father.

Use Psalm 149 to guide your praise for God.

1. Praise (Use Psalm 149 to guide you).

2. Gratitude (Use Psalm 149 to guide you).

3. Worship (Sing to Him).

4. Cry out to God with the lies you are believing and ask His forgiveness
(ACTS - Adoration, Confession, Thanksgiving, and Supplication).

5. Close your prayer time by quoting one of your verses back to God from memory. Hiding God's Word in your heart is a beautiful way to show God that you value Him and His thoughts.

6. Write out a closing prayer committing to believing God's truth alone.

4

Fear

4 Fear

Chapter 4 - Fear

Day 1

* Make sure to have your Bible, notebook, and pen.
* Pray before you start.
* Open your Bible and read the Scripture selected for today.
* Read Chapter 4 of <u>The Good Portion</u>.
* Begin learning your Scripture memory verse so you will be ready to recite it on Day 6.

Daily Scripture Reading - Matthew 14:22 – 33

Scripture Memory - Isaiah 41:10.

"Fear not, for I am with you; be not dismayed, for I am your God; I will strengthen you, I will help you, I will uphold you with my righteous right hand."

Chapter 4

What is it about open water, beaches, the crashing of waves, the cool breeze, and the magnificence and grandeur of the endless ocean on the horizon that intrigues us? We can sit for hours gazing upon the water and ponder the meaning of life, God, our past, our future, our struggles, our fears, our goals, and the purpose of it all.

A few years back, a group of us went on a cruise to celebrate my dad's seventy-fifth birthday. We were off on a fun-filled week's adventure down to the warm Caribbean Islands. Our cruise ship was a spectacular floating paradise. We had innumerable, delectable food choices and an array of activities to keep us busy 24/7. Stimulation overload for sure.

We all checked into our cabins, unpacked, and received our daily itineraries of activities and then we were called onto the deck for our muster drill before embarking on our voyage. We all learned how to put on our life jackets and where to go in case of an emergency.

After we were all prepped for any unexpected emergency, it was time to push back from the dock. We waved good-bye to a bunch of strangers, who all seemed to be waving back, and off we went on a grand adventure. We were now cruising out to sea toward the setting sun as it seemed to lead us out to the open waters.

We made our way to the elegant dining room, where we were served a mouth watering five-course meal. As we were finishing up our delightful dinner, we were informed by our maitre d' that a storm was approaching and would cause a bit of turbulence. Nothing to be terribly concerned about, just a cautionary note to watch our footing as we moved about the ship.

After dinner, we took a stroll around the deck, but soon we found it increasingly hard to walk around without falling over. The ship had now entered the awaited storm, and it was quickly apparent that we were in some very rough waters.

We were directed to go to our cabins and wait there while we weathered out the storm. From our cabin window, we could see the thirty-foot squalls crashing over the railings as the ship would list at about a thirty-degree angle from side to side. It felt as though we might tip over.

The winds were now at tropical-storm strength, and this had quickly turned into a serious situation. Over the loudspeaker, we heard one of the crew members announce that all passengers must be in their cabins with their life jackets on and wait there for further instructions.

We sat in our rooms looking out our windows as the hours passed. We prayed and asked God to calm the seas. He is the God of the universe and all nature submits to Him. We knew God would keep us safe, but I won't lie and tell you we weren't just a little bit scared. The thought of tipping over and drowning, being lost at sea, eaten by sharks, may have crossed our minds a few times. We knew that God was in control, but our eyes, emotions, and fear told us otherwise.

We finally did make it through the storm unscathed as the Lord calmed the seas. The crew did a great job getting everything back in order and we enjoyed the rest of our cruise, thanking God for His all-powerful hand over us.

Another group experienced the same nerve-racking ordeal as we did. The waves were crashing over their boat, the wind was howling, and it seemed certain they would capsize, just like we felt we would that night. Being helpless and feeling that you may die out at sea can certainly cause a lot of fear.

Peter, the disciple I most relate to, experienced this frightening night, just like I did on the cruise ship. However, his boat was quite a bit smaller and he had only a few cruisers with him. He definitely did not have all the delectable dishes delivered to his elegant cabin room. No, this was more in the line with a small working man's fishing boat.

> Being helpless and feeling that you may die out at sea can certainly cause a lot of fear.

Turn in your Bibles, stop and read Matthew 14:22–33. Jesus and the disciples had been serving thousands of people that day and they were excited as they saw Jesus performing miracles. The day was now over and everyone was exhausted. Jesus decided to go up in the mountains near the town of Capernaum, a beautiful city on the Sea of Galilee, to pray and spend quiet time with God.

Jesus instructed the disciples to get into a boat and meet Him later on the northwestern shore of the Sea of Galilee, which is about eight miles across. They obeyed joyfully. Today had been a full and wondrous day watching Jesus perform so many amazing miracles. They were enthusiastically talking about this memorable day that they would never forget … maybe.

As the disciples were rowing across the sea to the other side, they noticed a storm brewing off in the distance, much like my group and I noticed on our cruise. The wind picked up, the waves grew wilder, and before long they were in the midst of a serious storm.

A Ghost or...

They rowed frantically for three or four miles, which put them about halfway across the lake. Suddenly, one of the rowers saw something strange on the water. They all thought he was just delusional through exhaustion from rowing for hours. But another saw the odd figure as well. They immediately became frightened and wondered what it might be. How could anything be out here in this wild storm? Honestly, if I had seen a strange figure in the storm walking across the water while on our cruise ship, I might have been frightened as well.

One disciple said, "Is this an illusion from exhaustion, or is it a ghost?" But, just as they cried out in fear, they heard a call in a familiar voice that came from the figure on the water and said, "Take heart; it is I. Do not be afraid" (Matthew 14:27b). Fear is such a strong emotion that it can cause us to cry out loud in despair. The disciples felt fear like never before as their eyes moved between the storm and the "ghostly" figure. Jesus spoke like a parent calming a frightened child after a scary dream.

The ghostly voice sounded very familiar to the disciples and as the figure drew closer, they could now see that it was not a stranger but Jesus. But, their minds were confused. Had they forgotten that Jesus is God and can definitely walk on water? Peter doubted and wanted proof that it is not a ghost. He asked Jesus ...

"Lord, if it is You, command me to come to You on the water" (Matthew 14:28).

Why did Peter doubt? Well, we could ask the same question of ourselves. Why do we doubt His Word? Why do we need more proof of God? We have the entire Word of God to answer any doubt we may ever have. There are 66 Books, 1,189 chapters, 31,173 verses, and 807,361 of His holy inspired words. What is our excuse?

Now, Jesus could have scolded Peter for doubting, but He didn't. Like a loving father, He gently said, "Come" (Matthew 14:29). Peter, instantly dismissed his doubts, chose to ignore his feelings, took his eyes off the storm, and chose to obey. "So Peter got out of the boat, walked on the water and came to Jesus" (Matthew 14:29).

Peter chose to look to Jesus. His feelings told him to be fearful, look at the circumstances, not trust Jesus, and selfishly protect himself. Sinful fear always comes from a selfish, self-centered, self-protective heart. Sinful fear starts in the mind and takes root in our hearts.

The progression of sinful fear looks like this: We look away from our holy God — We doubt God — We look to our circumstances — We believe a lie — Fear takes root in our heart — We sinfully act on our fearful feelings. John Piper explains it so well:

> My feelings are not God. God is God. My feelings do not define truth. God's word defines truth. My feelings are echoes and responses to what my mind perceives. And sometimes—many times—my feelings are out of sync with the truth. When that happens—and it happens every day in some measure—I try not to bend the truth to justify my imperfect feelings, but rather, I plead with God: Purify my perceptions of your truth and transform my feelings so that they are in sync with the truth. [4]

Lost Focus

Peter trusted Jesus and was now out of the boat, literally walking on the water. Wow! As he fixed his eyes on Jesus and walked toward Him, he knew the truth and believed it was truly Jesus. Peter stared intently into Jesus's eyes as he walked toward the loving face of His Savior. He felt a sense of safety, calmness, and peace in the midst of the storm. His good and faithful Friend was right in front of him and it felt so right. That peace from Jesus is priceless in a storm. When is the last time you felt that kind of peace?

But something caught Peter's attention and distracted him. For a split second, he turned his eyes away from Jesus. He focused on the storm, the waves, the wind … on the circumstances around him. Peter forgot the goodness and power of Jesus, he was afraid, and he began to sink. But Jesus never took His eyes off of Peter. Peter took his eyes off of Jesus and feared for his life. "But when he saw the   wind, he was afraid, and beginning to sink, he cried out, 'Lord, save me'" (Matthew 14:30).

How many times have you been distracted by the circumstances in front of you, fearful, doubtful, forgetting God's faithfulness, not seeing the outstretched hand of Jesus, only finding yourself sinking into a bad situation, wishing for a way out? So many times we pray for God to change our circumstances, but we pray out of fear and selfishness for God to change things so we won't be afraid or uncomfortable. Our focus is on our feelings and not on the power of God to see us through the storm. Sinful fear is not about the feeling, it is about the sin.

Sinful fear is not about the feeling, it is about the sin.

Fear is sinful when:
You feel like the thing you fear has more power than God.
It is rooted in the loss of an idolatrous desire.
It is so paralyzing that it keeps us from fulfilling our biblical responsibilities.
It is rooted in selfishness rather than love.

The next verse is one of the most precious pictures of Jesus's fatherly love for His children. Jesus held out His hand to Peter. "Jesus immediately reached out his hand and took hold of him, saying to him, 'O you of little faith, why did you doubt'" (Matthew 14:31)?

Can't you just see Jesus standing there on the water, kindly holding out His hand to Peter, who wrestled with the fear of drowning? He knew what Peter was struggling with and He was right there offering His hand. Peter only needed to take it. Jesus holds out His hand to you as well. He sees what you are doing. He knows you're fearful, you struggle to maintain control, protecting yourself, and focused on your circumstances. But He kindly stands there waiting for you to take His hand. He always offers His love, mercy, grace, joy, protection, comfort, and peace, but we must be willing to trust Him in the midst of our circumstances.

With God, I am Safe!

Peter and Jesus walked together back to the boat through the storm. That is such a picture of God's love for us. When Jesus and Peter got into the boat, the seas immediately calmed. Jesus wanted Peter to know He would always be there in the storms of life. We know that Peter would face many more storms in the future.
"And when they got into the boat, the wind ceased. And those in the boat worshiped him, saying, 'Truly, You are the Son of God'" (Matthew 14:33).

The disciples finally got it. They acknowledged that Jesus is God and they worshipped Him. Their focus was back where it needed to be. He is the only place we must run in the storms of life. God must be the only One to whom we run. Timothy Keller describes it best,

> My fears are directly proportional to the vulnerability of the things
> that are my greatest joys. If the thing that is my greatest joy is God,
> I will live without fear. If my one thing … the thing I most want …
> is God, I am safe.[5]

David got it: "One thing have I asked of the Lord, that will I seek after: that I may dwell in the house of the Lord all the days of my life, to gaze upon the beauty of the Lord and to inquire in his temple" (Psalm 27:4).

We must desire "one thing" like David, to be in the presence of God. That is where fear cannot reside. Let's say this together with the disciples: "Truly, You are the Son of God."

Choose the one necessary thing ⋯ the Good Portion. Choose to worship only God!

Reflection:

◆ Stop and pray right now and ask God to graciously and kindly reveal your fears and the lies that you believe.

◆ Write a list of the fears that come to mind. What do you fear losing or experiencing? Are there people you fear? Who and why? Whose approval are you afraid of not receiving? Why?

◆ One by one, acknowledge these sinful fears to God. Humbly confess these to God. Then ask for His gracious forgiveness for each fear. Humbly ask God to forgive you for choosing to worship another god. I John 1: 9 tells us He promises to forgive us immediately when we ask.

◆ You can be free from the bondage of these idols right now through the power of God in Christ Jesus. Freedom in Christ is graciously offered to you this very moment. Whom will you choose to worship?

Day 2 - Fear

* Make sure to have your Bible, Companion Journal, and pen.
* Pray before you start. Use the guided prayer.
* Open your Bible and read the Scripture selected for today.
* Begin learning your Scripture memory verse and review it throughout the week.

Prayer: Use this prayer as a guide.

> *Loving Father, I come to You with a humble heart. I carry the load of fear and worry. I need You to help me see the sin of my heart, the distrust, the doubt, and the lies I so easily believe. Father, I want to be free from the fear that is gripping me. I can only be free through Your power to break the bondage of the sin in my heart. I need the boldness to release my control to You. I need Your power over my fear and my past circumstances that I allow to hold me captive. May I have Your wisdom and insight to see You as You are. God, all-powerful, mighty, and worthy to be worshipped alone. In Jesus's powerful name, Amen.*

Recite your Scripture Memory - Isaiah 41:10.

"Fear not, for I am with you; be not dismayed, for I am your God; I will strengthen you, I will help you, I will uphold you with my righteous right hand."

Open your Bible to Matthew 14:22 – 33. Read these verses.

Day 2 Questions - Use your Companion Journal to answer the questions.

1. Describe the scene given to us in Matthew 14: 13–21. List all of the ways Jesus showed kindness.

2. In Matthew 14: 22, why did Jesus dismiss the crowds and choose to go alone to the mountain?

3. Why is it important for us to do the same as Jesus did in Matthew 14: 22?

4. How often do you get alone with God? How much time do you spend in quiet, undistracted time with God? What are the things that keep you from spending time with Him?

Meditate on Isaiah 41:10.

"Fear not, for I am with you; be not dismayed, for I am your God; I will strengthen you, I will help you, I will uphold you with my righteous right hand."

Close this time in grateful worship and prayer.

Day 3 - Fear

* Make sure to have your Bible, Companion Journal, and pen.

* Pray before you start. Use the guided prayer.

* Open your Bible and read the Scripture selected for today.

* Begin learning your Scripture memory verse and review it throughout the week.

Prayer: Use this prayer as a guide.

God, truly You are the Son of God. You are the God of the universe who calms the storms. You call out for me in the midst of my own storm, my rebellion, doubt, mistrust, and forgetfulness. God, please help me to see You in all Your holiness, mercy, and grace. I need Your hand in my life to set me free from the bondage of fear. Perfect love casts out fear. I need to feel Your perfect love in my life. Thank You for loving me. In the mighty name of Jesus, Amen.

Recite your Scripture Memory - Isaiah 41:10.

"Fear not, for I am with you; be not dismayed, for I am your God; I will strengthen you, I will help you, I will uphold you with my righteous right hand."

Open your Bible to Matthew 14:22 – 33. Read these verses.

Day 3 Questions - Use your Companion Journal to answer the questions.

1. Describe what you think the disciples must have felt as the storm descended upon them.

2. What is your greatest storm right now and what brings fear when you think about that?

3. What does Philippians 4: 6-7 tell us to do with our fears? If we obey verse 6, what does verse 7 tell us we will receive?

4. How do the thoughts in your mind lead to the fears in your heart and encourage the greatest anxiety and worry?

Meditate on Philippians 4:6 – 7.

"Do not be anxious about anything, but in everything by prayer and supplication with thanksgiving let your requests be made known to God. And the peace of God, which surpasses all understanding, will guard your hearts and your minds in Christ Jesus."

Close this time in grateful worship and prayer.

Day 4 - Fear

* Make sure to have your Bible, Companion Journal, and pen.
* Pray before you start. Use the guided prayer.
* Open your Bible and read the Scripture reading for today.
* Begin learning your Scripture memory verse and review it throughout the week.

Prayer: Use this prayer as a guide.

> *Father, You tell me in Your Word not to be anxious about anything, but I need Your power to overcome my fears. Help me to believe that You are powerful enough to rescue me from all my fears. You promise me Your peace will guard my heart and mind. I desperately need that. Help me to surrender my fears to You, the only One who is able to give me perfect peace. Thank You, Father. In the priceless name of Jesus, Amen.*

Recite your Scripture Memory - Isaiah 41:10.

"Fear not, for I am with you; be not dismayed, for I am your God; I will strengthen you, I will help you, I will uphold you with my righteous right hand."

Open your Bible to Matthew 14:22 – 33. Read these verses.

Day 4 Questions - Use yourCompanion Journal to answer the questions.

1. Read Matthew 14: 25. Why do you think Jesus came to them on the water?

2. Why were the disciples scared when they saw Jesus on the water, and what did they do?

3. When is the last time you cried to God out of fear?

4. Why does God want to rescue you from your fears?

Meditate on 1 Peter 5:6 – 7.

"Humble yourselves, therefore, under the mighty hand of God so that at the proper time he may exalt you, casting all your anxieties on him, because he cares for you."

Close this time in grateful worship and prayer.

Day 5 - Fear

* Make sure to have your Bible, Companion Journal, and pen.
* Pray before you start. Use the guided prayer.
* Open your Bible and read the Scripture selected for today.
* Begin learning your Scripture memory verse and review it throughout the week.

Prayer: Use this prayer as a guide.

> *Dear Father, I am coming before You today with my fears. I desire to be free of the bondage of fear. I know that only You can free me and give me victory over my lack of trust in who You are. Help me to trust in Your faithfulness and steadfast love for me. May Your love chase away all my fears and the control I give to my fears. I want to surrender to Your mighty power in my life. You are love! Open my eyes to the truth of my heart. Thank You. In the kind and merciful name of Jesus, Amen.*

Recite your Scripture Memory - Isaiah 41:10.

"Fear not, for I am with you; be not dismayed, for I am your God; I will strengthen you, I will help you, I will uphold you with my righteous right hand."

Open your Bible to Matthew 14:22 – 33. Read these verses.

Day 5 Questions - Use your Companion Journal to answer the questions.

1. In Matthew 14: 27, what did Jesus say to the disciples?

2. Why does Jesus say to Peter, "Oh you of little faith, why do you doubt?"

3. What happened in Matthew 14: 30 and why is this important?

4. Why is it hard to give up your fears and trust God?

5. What are the attributes of God that bring you the greatest comfort?

Meditate on Psalm 91:1, 2.

"He who dwells in the shelter of the Most High will abide in the shadow of the Almighty. I will say to the Lord, 'My refuge and my fortress, my God, in whom I trust.'"

Close this time in grateful worship and prayer.

Day 6 The Good Portion - A Time of Worship

This is the day of the week that you do as Mary did and sit for an extended amount of time in prayer and worship. Block out at least an hour, perhaps more, once a week, to have extended time to be still, sit quietly all by yourself, and simply worship your Father.

Use Psalm 91 to guide your praise for God.

1. Praise (Use Psalm 91 to guide you).

2. Gratitude (Use Psalm 91 to guide you).

3. Worship (Sing).

4. Pray (ACTS - Adoration, Confession, Thanksgiving, and Supplication).

5. Quoting one of your verses back to God from memory will help seal it in your mind. Hiding God's Word in your heart is a beautiful way to show God that you value Him and His thoughts.

6. Write out a closing prayer committing to trust in God's love.

5

Idols

5 Idols

Chapter 5 - Idols

Day 1

* Make sure to have your Bible, Companion Journal, and pen.
* Pray before you start.
* Open your Bible and read the Scripture selected for today.
* Read Chapter 5 of The Good Portion.
* Begin learning your Scripture memory verse so you will be ready to recite it on Day 6.

Daily Scripture Reading - Exodus 1 / Deuteronomy 8

Scripture Memory - Psalm 95:1

"Oh come, let us sing to the Lord; let us make a joyful noise to the rock of our salvation! Let us come into his presence with thanksgiving; let us make a joyful noise to him with songs of praise! For the Lord is a great God, and a great King above all gods."

Chapter 5

Thousands of candles glistened and reflected off of the beautifully handcrafted crystal chandeliers. Shimmers of light flickered everywhere. All the majestic royal carriages were streaming in one by one, circling the long front drive of the grand palace entrance.

Each nobleman was dressed in his best regal attire, while each lady wore a custom-designed, elegant gown, flowing with rich lace and sparkling gems. But as beautiful as each gown was, the protocol was to never outshine the queen herself. This would be considered an extreme social faux pas.

The royal banquet was being celebrated in honor of the new king of Egypt, who had just arrived earlier that week to secure his royal crown and place on the throne. There was so much excitement in the kingdom. A new dynasty was now in place with a mysterious king from a faraway land that was going to be crowned the new leader of Egypt.

Beautiful music filled the air in every room of the palace that day. Skilled musicians played a unique array of instruments; harps, lutes, drums, tambourines, pipes, and clappers for the arriving honored guests. Dozens of singers and dancers, personally selected by the king, roamed the palace mesmerizing and entertaining guests as they mingled about.

All at once, it became completely quiet. No one seemed to move a muscle. The loud ceremonial fanfare of brass trumpets abruptly sounded, announcing the entrance of someone quite important. Everyone turned towards the east to face the grand golden staircase and witness the royal entrance of the mysterious new king and his elegant and beautiful wife. Their presence at the top of the stairs demanded a sense of respect and honor as the royal couple waited to be properly introduced to their palace guests. A strong, loud, commanding voice declared,

"All rise! A royal proclamation is declared on this day in history, an imperial decree to be sent out to all the regions, kingdoms and lands, that Egypt's prior monarchy is forever removed and a new sovereign king has secured the throne. I now present to you Pharaoh, King of Egypt, and his royal queen."

The graceful queen took the strong arm of her mighty king. They majestically glided down the elegant, golden, handcrafted staircase, taking slow, methodical steps. Every prince, princess, nobleman, and lady bowed or curtsied in humble respect for the new rulers of their kingdom. As the royal couple made their way to the banquet room, their guests had to wait. Once they were seated at their table, everyone else was escorted to their assigned seats to join them. With this, the festivities began. The bountiful feast was grander than anyone could have imagined. Exotic meats such as ducks, geese, pigeons, and various other birds were offered. An abundance of imported red wines from regions far away was served to each honored guest. It was a grand and glorious royal banquet to remember for a lifetime.

Royal Dynasty Secure

The king, now on the throne, gave all Egyptians a sense of safety and security. Life would get better as the new king met with his governors and chief assistants to make plans for how he would rule the kingdom.

Open your Bibles to Exodus 1, where we find our king, the king of Eighteenth Dynasty Egypt (1550–1295 BC), proclaiming his first order of business. He commanded that all of his soldiers check on the foreigners living in Egypt (the Israelites) and report back to him quickly. He had recently learned that these folks were the Israelites originally from Canaan.

> I think we have all been fearful of losing something we treasure.

Something bothered him about these immigrants. They made him nervous. He began to worry. He could see that they were great in number, they were skilled workers, they were prosperous, diligent, strong, and fruitful, and they might rise up against the king and throw him off the throne. Exodus 1:7 tells us, "But the people of Israel were fruitful and increased greatly; they multiplied and grew exceedingly strong so that the land was filled with them."

Stan and Sylvia

Have you ever felt like the king? I have. I think we have all been fearful of losing something we treasure. A sweet woman (I will call her Sylvia) whom I counseled a few years back feared losing her husband, Stan. Now, my husband and I knew Stan to be godly, loyal, upright, and loving. He had never given one indication that he would ever be unfaithful to his wife, but she thought up many unrealistic scenarios where he might leave her and reject her as his wife.

Sylvia conjured up thoughts of Stan abandoning their marriage and running off with another woman, but his actions always proved his faithfulness. He truly loved his wife and that was evident to everyone but Sylvia. Every day she would demand to know everything thing he did and who he was with and questioned his every move. When I asked Sylvia about her relationship with God, her answer was enlightening: "I try to spend time alone with God, but before I realize it, my busy day gets the best of me."

During our first couple of meetings, I could see where Sylvia's treasures were, what her obsessions were, and where she placed her fears. She would often say, "I just don't know what I'd do if Stan left me. I just can't live without him. I don't want to be left alone without a husband." She had made her marriage an idol. She lived in her marriage with gripping fear.

Well, Sylvia and the king of Egypt had a similar problem. The king feared losing his position on the throne and Sylvia feared losing her position as Stan's wife. The Israelites had no intention of overthrowing the throne, and Stan had no intention of getting a new wife.

The perceived threats for both the king and Sylvia were built out of fears, doubt, and lies. They allowed fear to take root in their hearts, began to doubt, believed lies, then devised plans to safeguard what they feared losing. Tim Keller puts it this way, "There is no possibility of our worshiping nothing. Since we need to worship something, because of how we are created, we cannot eliminate God without creating God-substitutes. Something will capture our hearts and imaginations, becoming the most important concern, value, or allegiance in our lives. So every personality, community, and thought will be based on either God Himself or some god-substitute, an idol."[6]

A Cry for Rescue

The most important thing to the king was his throne, and he would let no one stand in the way of him having what he so desperately desired. Sadly, that meant the Israelites would spend the next 430 years in slavery to the Egyptians. The king worshipped a god—himself.

After many years, this king died. Many kings came after him, and they continued to keep the Israelites in slavery. Finally, at the end of 430 years of slavery, the Israelites cried out to God for redemption and rescue from their slavery.

"And the people of Israel groaned because of their slavery and cried out for help. Their cry for rescue from slavery came up to God. And God heard their groaning, and God remembered his covenant with Abraham, with Isaac, and with Jacob. God saw the people of Israel—and God knew" (Exodus 2:22, 23).

They started to doubt God's goodness, started to question His plan

God heard their cry and would free them from slavery. But who would God use to lead them out of slavery? An unlikely man, the son of the Pharaoh. Moses, an Israelite baby adopted and raised by Egyptian royalty, would lead his people out of bondage to freedom.

God used Moses as their redemptive leader and graciously led the Israelites out of bondage to freedom to the desert, where He would lovingly take care of His people for forty years. He fed them with manna daily, provided springs of fresh water that flowed out of rocks, led them by a cloud, and did miracle after miracle, showing loving kindness to His people. God had made a covenant and would be faithful to His promise.

But after wandering in the desert for years, the people became disillusioned with roaming, and the daily manna became boring. They started to doubt God's goodness, started to question His plan, and wondered if He really knew what He was doing.

The Israelites became impatient waiting for Moses to come down the mountain with more instructions. They feared their life in the desert would never end, and they doubted God's worthiness. They wanted the freedom to make their own rules, fulfill the desires of their flesh, ignore the moral laws, and just live it up. So, they looked to other gods to give them what they wanted. The people made idols and worshipped them instead.

> "When the people saw that Moses delayed to come down from the mountain, the people gathered themselves together to Aaron and said to him, "Up, make us gods who shall go before us. As for this Moses, the man who brought us up out of the land of Egypt, we do not know what has become of him." So Aaron said to them, "Take off the rings of gold that are in the ears of your wives, your sons, and your daughters, and bring them to me." So all the people took off the rings of gold that were in their ears and brought them to Aaron. And he received the gold from their hand and fashioned it with a graving tool and made a golden calf. And they said, "These are your gods, O Israel, who brought you up out of the land of Egypt!" Exodus 32:1

Every time I read the story of the Israelites, I am baffled. I think to myself, why? Why are they so forgetful? Why is God so patient with them? Why does He put up with all their rebellion? How could they make idols and worship other gods after all that the true God had done for them?

The answer will bring tears to your eyes ...

"For you are a people holy to the Lord your God. The Lord your God has chosen you to be a people for his treasured possession, out of all the peoples who are on the face of the earth." Deuteronomy 7:6

Did you hear that? God calls them His TREASURED POSSESSION! They worship idols, turn their backs on Him, grumble, and complain and in return God says He loves them and treasures them! And as if that's not enough, read what else he says about His treasured people:

Forgetful Promises

> "It was not because you were more in number than any other people that the Lord set his love on you and chose you, for you were the fewest of all peoples, but it is because the Lord loves you and is keeping the oath that he swore to your fathers, that the Lord has brought you out with a mighty hand and redeemed you from the house of slavery, from the hand of Pharaoh king of Egypt. Know therefore that the Lord your God is God, the faithful God who keeps covenant and steadfast love with those who love him and keep his commandments, to a thousand generations." Deuteronomy 7:7–9

Wow! Never once does God mention their actions as gaining them some right to God's choosing them, redeeming them, loving them, or calling them holy or treasured. No, it was God alone who made a covenant to Abraham, Isaac, and Jacob to redeem the Israelites, and He keeps His promise to a thousand generations because He is God!

The Israelites chose to forget the promises of God, look away from the Truth, doubt God, and believe a lie. They looked to a worthless idol to fulfill their flesh, and sinful actions followed.

> Idolatry...includes anything on which we set our affections and indulge as an excessive and sinful attachment... Idolatry includes anything we worship: the lust for pleasure, respect, love, power, control, or freedom from pain. Furthermore, the problem is not outside of us, located in a liquor store or on the Internet; the problem is within us. Alcohol and drugs are essentially satisfiers of deeper idols. The problem is not with the idolatrous substance; it is the false worship of the heart.[7]

Fear — Doubt — Lies —Idols— Sinful Action

> The purpose of all idolatry is to manipulate the idol for our own benefit. This means that we don't want to be ruled by idols. Instead, we want to use them... Idolaters want nothing above themselves, including their idols. Their fabricated gods are intended to be mere puppet kings, means to an end... Idols, however, do not cooperate. Rather than mastering our idols, we

become enslaved by them and begin to look like them. As idols are deaf, dumb, blind, utterly senseless, and irrational, so "those who make them will be like them, and so will all who trust in them" (Psalm 115:8). How can these lifeless idols exert so much power? They dominate because of a powerful but quiet presence that hides behind every idol, Satan himself.[8]

Idols are anything we treasure more than God. Anything we think we need to feel loved, valued, accepted, or secure. Idols are the root motivation of our pride, envy, fear, and self-worship. Anything we put in place of God is an idol. Even good things can be turned into idols when we look to them to satisfy what only God can fulfill in us. David Powlison writes:

> Anything we put in place of God is an idol.

> The most basic question which God continually poses to each human heart [is]: Has something or someone besides Jesus the Christ taken title to your heart's trust, preoccupation, loyalty, service, fear, and delight? It is a question bearing on the immediate motivation of one's behavior, thoughts, and feelings. In the Bible's conceptualization, the motivation question is the lordship question: who or what 'rules' my behavior, the Lord or an idol?[9]

> Ask yourself these questions:
> What do I think about most?
> What do I do with my time?
> Who do I want to most mimic?
> Whose opinion do I care most about?
> What can't I live without?

If I'm not careful, even writing this book can become an idol for me. I can make it an obsession, using it to gain approval, to receive accolades, to reach a goal, or to fulfill a longing. It can consume my every thought. If I'm not careful, this book can quickly become something I worship in the place of God. Elise Fitzpatrick reminds us that, "These idols of our hearts are the desires, ideals, or expectations that we worship, serve, and long for."[10]

How do I safeguard myself from allowing this book to become an idol? By focusing on God's attributes, acknowledging His faithfulness, His goodness, His steadfastness, and His promises and humbly acknowledging my weakness in doing anything without His power. This book must be written to glorify God and Him alone. David reminds me of this in Psalm 97:9: "For You, O Lord, are the Most High over all the earth; You are exalted far above all gods." Idols are a trap. They enslave us. They demand to be worshipped. They lie to us. They promise to satisfy. They are relentless. They will destroy us.

> What is most important to us? What do we love? What is most dear to us? We shouldn't be surprised that these questions get to the core of our being. They also point to where we are headed. All roads eventually lead to our relationship with God. Do we love what he loves? Is he most dear to us?[11]

Our king, at the beginning of this chapter, had an obsession to be worshipped as king on the throne. He did whatever it took to make that happen, even enslaving thousands of Israelites. For 430 years, they were slaves to the Egyptians.

God, through His grace, redeemed them, replenished them, and restored them, but after a time, they forgot, turned from God, and began to worship idols that continually enslaved them. They were only content, fulfilled, and at peace when God was the only One they worshipped.

God has redeemed you through the blood of His Son, Jesus Christ, to live in freedom. Galatians 5:1 says, "For freedom, Christ has set us free; stand firm therefore, and do not submit again to a yoke of slavery." You are free! You are His treasured possession! He brings total satisfaction, joy, peace, and contentment. No worthless idol of your heart will ever treasure you!

Deuteronomy 7:6 says, "The Lord your God has chosen you to be a people for his treasured possession, out of all the peoples who are on the face of the earth."

Are you choosing to live like a slave and bow down to the idols of your heart? Idols are a cheap, fake substitution for God and will not EVER satisfy. How sad that we choose to replace Him in our hearts with fake, worthless gods ... gods that will never treasure us.

Created to Worship

He treasures you! Do you treasure Him? Do you value Him? Do you humbly worship Him and Him alone? The answer is easy to figure out. How much do you think about Him, spend time with Him, worship Him, meditate on His word? How many Scriptures can you recite right now off the top of your head? What are you treasuring in your heart?

Remember, we were created to worship. What are you worshipping?

Exodus 20:1–3 says, "And God spoke all these words, saying, 'I am the Lord your God, who brought you out of the land of Egypt, out of the house of slavery. You shall have no other gods before me.'"
God told the Israelites the same thing He tells us: Have NO other Gods! Have NO IDOLS! You will worship what you treasure.

Choose the one necessary thing ⋯ the Good Portion. Choose to worship only God!

Reflection:

✦ Stop and pray right now and ask God to graciously and kindly reveal the idols of your heart, the idols that you value and treasure more than Him.

✦ Write a list of the idols that come to mind. Think of every person, possession, position, ideal, desire, or expectation and ask yourself if you could live without that particular thing.

✦ One by one, acknowledge the idol you have been worshipping. Confess these to God. Then ask for His gracious forgiveness for each idol. Humbly ask God to forgive you for choosing to worship another god. I John 1: 9 tells us He promises to forgive us immediately when we ask.

✦ You can be free from the bondage of these idols right now through the power of God in Christ Jesus. Freedom in Christ is graciously offered to you this very moment. Whom will you choose to worship?

Day 2 - Idols

* Make sure to have your Bible, Companion Journal, and pen.
* Pray before you start. Use the guided prayer.
* Open your Bible and read the Scripture selected for today.
* Begin learning your Scripture memory verse and review it throughout the week.

Prayer: Use this prayer as a guide.

Holy Father, You alone are worthy to be worshipped. I praise You because You are holy. I know that You tell me in Your Word that You alone are to be worshipped. I ask You to reveal the idols of my heart to which I am blinded. Search my heart and show me the things that I value more than You. Thank You for loving me and treasuring me. In Jesus's holy name, Amen.

Recite your Scripture Memory - Psalm 95:1.

"Oh come, let us sing to the Lord; let us make a joyful noise to the rock of our salvation! Let us come into his presence with thanksgiving; let us make a joyful noise to him with songs of praise! For the Lord is a great God, and a great King above all gods."

Open your Bible to Deuteronomy 8. Read the entire chapter once.

Day 2 Questions - Use your Companion Journal to answer the questions.

1. After the Israelites had wandered in the desert for forty years, Deuteronomy 8 shows us that God gave them a charge to not forget all that the Lord had done before they entered the Promised Land.

2. Why did He do this?

3. Why do we so easily forget the faithfulness and goodness of God?

4. Why do you think the First Commandment is "You shall have no other gods before me?" (Exodus 20: 3)

5. What are the idols in your life that distract you from spending time alone, quietly worshipping God?

Meditate on Exodus 15:11.

"Who is like you, O Lord, among the gods? Who is like you, Majestic in Holiness, Awesome in glorious deeds, doing wonders?"

Close this time in grateful worship and prayer.

Day 3 - Idols

* Make sure to have your Bible, Companion Journal, and pen.
* Pray before you start. Use the guided prayer.
* Open your Bible and read the Scripture selected for today.
* Begin learning your Scripture memory verse and review it throughout the week.

Prayer: Use this prayer as a guide.

> *God my God, holy, holy, holy! I humbly come before You remembering Your faithfulness, Your goodness, and Your mercy. Open my eyes to any idols that I am replacing You with. Help me see my heart the way You see it. Please give me insight into Your Word right now. In Jesus's mighty name, Amen.*

Recite your Scripture Memory - Psalm 95:1.

"Oh come, let us sing to the Lord; let us make a joyful noise to the rock of our salvation! Let us come into his presence with thanksgiving; let us make a joyful noise to him with songs of praise! For the Lord is a great God, and a great King above all gods."

Open your Bible to Deuteronomy 8. Read the entire chapter once.

Day 3 Questions - Use your Companion Journal to answer the questions.

1. Count how many times God says, "forget" or "remember" in chapter 8.
Why do you think God repeats this so many times?

2. In what ways do you see God taking care of the Israelites?
In what ways does He take care of you?

3. Why does God take idols so seriously?

4. How can you find more time to worship Him? To what will you be willing to commit?
Why or why not?

Meditate on Psalm 117:1, 2.

"Praise the Lord, all nations! Extol him, all peoples! For great is his steadfast love toward us, and the faithfulness of the Lord endures forever. Praise the Lord!"

Close this time in grateful worship and prayer.

Day 4 - Idols

* Make sure to have your Bible, Companion Journal, and pen.
* Pray before you start. Use the guided prayer.
* Open your Bible and read the Scripture selected for today.
* Begin learning your Scripture memory verse and review it throughout the week.

Prayer: Use this prayer as a guide.

> *Father, Psalm 117:2 says, "For great is His steadfast love toward us, and the faithfulness of the Lord endures forever." I praise You because You are steadfast and faithful. I worship You because You are worthy. I come humbly to You and ask You to please give me Your wisdom right now and help my heart to be open to the Holy Spirit. In Jesus's powerful name, Amen.*

Recite your Scripture Memory - Psalm 95:1.

"Oh come, let us sing to the Lord; let us make a joyful noise to the rock of our salvation! Let us come into his presence with thanksgiving; let us make a joyful noise to him with songs of praise! For the Lord is a great God, and a great King above all gods."

Open your Bible to Deuteronomy 8. Read the entire chapter once.

Day 4 Questions - Use your Companion Journal to answer the questions.

1. Read verse Deuteronomy 8: 3. What truths do you see in this verse?

2. Why is the Word of the Lord so important?

3. Can we worship only one thing?

4. Idols are things we worship more than God. Finish this statement: "I can't live without_____"

Now surrender that idol or those idols to the Lord. Confess your sin and humbly ask for forgiveness. Worship Him with gratitude.

Meditate on Isaiah 44:6.

"Thus says the Lord, the King of Israel and his Redeemer, the Lord of hosts 'I am the first and I am the last; besides me there is no god.'"

Close this time in grateful worship and prayer.

Day 5 - Worship God Only

✱ Make sure to have your Bible, Companion Journal, and pen.

✱ Pray before you start. Use the guided prayer.

✱ Open your Bible and read the Scripture selected for today.

✱ Begin learning your Scripture memory verse and review it throughout the week.

Prayer: Use this prayer as a guide.

> *Dear God, thank You for allowing me the privilege and honor to call You my Father. I am eternally grateful to You for sanctifying me and covering me in Jesus's righteousness. I am forever your child and can never lose my position in Christ. Your Word is truth and is unshakable. It is the authority on which I stand. I love You and praise You in the name of Jesus, Amen.*

Recite your Scripture Memory - Psalm 95:1.

"Oh come, let us sing to the Lord; let us make a joyful noise to the rock of our salvation! Let us come into his presence with thanksgiving; let us make a joyful noise to him with songs of praise! For the Lord is a great God, and a great King above all gods".

Open your Bible to Deuteronomy 8. Read the entire chapter once.

Day 5 Questions - Use your Companion Journal to answer the questions.

1. Define what an idol is.

2. If you are not worshipping God, what other things might you be worshipping and why?

3. Why does Paul give us this warning in Romans 8: "Those who live according to the flesh set their minds on the things of the flesh, but those who live according to the Spirit set their minds on the things of the Spirit. To set the mind on the flesh is death, but to set the mind on the Spirit is life and peace?" (Romans 8: 5-6)

4. Go back to the list of probable idols you might be struggling with and list some of them here. Identify and surrender each idol as you write them. Ask God to forgive you for worshipping these idols.

Meditate on Hebrews 10:22 – 23.

"Let us draw near with a true heart in full assurance of faith, with our hearts sprinkled clean from an evil conscience and our bodies washed with pure water. Let us hold fast the confession of our hope without wavering, for he who promised is faithful."

Close this time in grateful worship and prayer.

Day 6 - The Good Portion - A Time of Worship

This is the day of the week that you do as Mary did and sit for an extended amount of time in prayer and worship. Block out at least an hour, perhaps more, to have extended time to be still, sit quietly all by yourself, and simply worship your Father.

Use Psalm 116 to guide your praise for God.

1. Praise (Use Psalm 116 to guide you).

2. Gratitude (Use Psalm 116 to guide you).

3. Worship.

4. Cry out to God with your joys, hurts, sadness, pain, guilt, shame, and repentance.

5. Close your prayer time by quoting one of your verses back to God from memory. Hiding God's Word in your heart is a beautiful way to show God that you value Him and His thoughts.

6. Write out a closing prayer committing to believing God is God alone.

6
Bitterness

6 Bitterness

Chapter 6 - Bitterness

Day 1

* Make sure to have your Bible, Companion Journal, and pen.
* Pray before you start.
* Open your Bible and read the Scripture selected for today.
* Read Chapter 6 of The Good Portion.
* Begin learning your Scripture memory verse so you will be ready to recite it on Day 6.

Daily Scripture Reading - Psalm 51

Scripture Memory - Psalm 51:1, 2.

"Have mercy on me, O God, according to Your steadfast love; according to Your abundant mercy blot out my transgressions. Wash me thoroughly from my iniquity, and cleanse me from my sin!"

Chapter 6

- I can never forgive him for what he did! Ever!!
- I grit my teeth every time her name is mentioned.
- Why did God allow that to happen to me? I can't forgive Him.
- She has hurt me for too many years, I'll never be able to forgive her.
- After all these years he comes begging for forgiveness. Nope, Sorry.
- I see no reason to forgive her, she'll just do it again.
- He died years ago and what's the point forgiving him now?
- She needs to show much more remorse or I won't forgive her.
- Why should I forgive him? He doesn't realize how hurt I am.

The gritting of teeth, the knot in your stomach, the angry eyebrows, all come into play when you hear the mention of that person's name. Maybe you even feel a little satisfaction when you hear that this person fell on hard times or is going through a rough trial. You secretly rejoice. You think about forgiving this person, but you just can't. Why is it so hard to forgive? Why should we forgive? How do we forgive? Have you ever asked these questions?

Maybe you've felt like this … "I forgave the person who hurt me a dozen times, but then I find myself gritting my teeth as I remember that particular incident years ago. I just can't stop thinking about it. It instantly makes me so angry."

Playing that scene over and over in your head is enough to drive you insane. You try to stop the thoughts, but they just keep coming. Sadly, we have all been there at some point in our lives. It can feel like a prison in which we are trapped. We desperately want to be freed … or do we?

Cindy

I met Cindy at church years ago. We had the normal, cordial, and polite chitchat, but, I could tell that Cindy looked tired and spoke with a sad tone. I felt God prompting me to invite her for coffee. I said, "Cindy, I would love to grab coffee this week if you have some time. I'd love to get to know you better and hear more of your testimony." We exchanged numbers and a few days later I received a text from her. She said that my invitation was an answer to prayer. She had a lot on her heart and would love to meet and share with me. I decided to invite her to my home on a night that my family would be gone. I felt she might open up more if she wasn't in the middle of a crowded coffee shop.

That following Friday, I opened the door to my home and there stood Cindy right on time. I could tell immediately that she came with a load of cares on her shoulders. She looked tired and thoroughly exhausted. She had a downcast look and sadness in her eyes as she mustered up a forced but polite smile. As we sat in my living room, I prayed for our time together. I wasn't even halfway through my prayer when Cindy began to sob. She was such a broken woman.

I asked, "Cindy, can you share what's on your heart?" The floodgates opened and all the hurt flowed out. She was so discouraged. She felt trapped in her circumstances and didn't know where to go. She wanted to feel free from the weight of her problems. She began by telling me about her husband, Peter, which was the topic of our conversation for the first forty minutes. The next twenty were spent on her "disrespectful, disobedient" children. Her tone was angry as she enlightened me about her three children (ages ten, fourteen, and seventeen) and the lack of respect and honor they showed her and Peter.

> She felt trapped in her circumstances and didn't know where to go.

Throughout our two-and-a-half-hour meeting, I showered Cindy with compassion, understanding, kindness, tears, love, hugs, and a listening ear. I let her know that I truly cared for her broken heart, hurts, and discouragements.

I believed that aside from her circumstance, there was an amazing woman who needed to know the God who could free her and give her the love, peace, hope, and freedom she was so desperately seeking. She needed to be reminded of her faithful Father and all of His amazing promises.

I then asked her questions about her faith in Jesus and concluded by her answers that she was a believer. I asked about Peter's faith and concluded that he was a believer as well (he had trusted Christ as his Savior in college).

Cindy admitted that her relationship with God was weak. She was not in the Word as often as she would like, but would pray and read her Bible when she had time. However, much of her time was spent on more materialistic endeavors, like her love for shopping, which helped distract her from her sad circumstances. She had a real obsession for shoes and jewelry and her online shopping was out of control. This all led to a lot of arguing between her and Peter.

"You're the one to talk"

Cindy went on to tell me how she was crying out for love and affection in her marriage and Peter was not interested in providing it. She thought he was purposely withholding his affection in order to punish her. He was insensitive, was lacking in his leadership responsibilities, was angry much of the time, and sometimes wouldn't even talk to her.

The kids were emotionally distant and retreated to their bedrooms for hours after school. They argued with one another over who touched something of theirs or dared to step foot in the other's room. They were ugly, rude, sarcastic, and vindictive with one another. Either they would all hide in their individual, separate bedrooms or they would leave to hang out with their friends.

Cindy said she was trying her best to be a good wife and mother, but felt so alone and unappreciated. She tried to help Peter see how he was damaging their marriage and she pled with him to seek help. She yelled, cried, and begged for him to change, but he just walked away. She had confronted Peter many times about his anger and he always responded with, "You're the one to talk … you're always yelling and stomping around, slamming doors, just to let everyone know how mad you are."

She says her husband was just so mean to her. Cindy said, "Of course I get angry. He makes me so mad. No one could live with this man. I see other husbands being kind and loving to their wives and I wish Peter would act like that."

I asked Cindy about her growing-up years. She grew up with only one parent. Her father left when she was six. She said, "My dad completely abandoned me and I just can't forgive him for doing that. I never had a decent role model, because my mom was gone a lot and we didn't spend any time together."

Cindy was forced to stay with her grandma during the day while her mom was at work. She was kind to Cindy and led her to a salvation decision at the age of ten. Cindy's words at this point were spoken through gritted teeth, with squinty eyes, and her tone was much louder. She said, "I feel that I am doing the best I can in this marriage. I'm not perfect, but what can you expect?" She did admit that Peter had changed for the better recently and he was trying to be a better husband, but it was a little late for that. She also admitted he had asked for her forgiveness for his past sins against her. "It's just been too many years of pain, I will never be able to forgive him."

Cindy's story is a sad one. It makes my heart break for her and many like her, trapped in a heart of bitterness, anger, and hopelessness. Cindy is a precious woman, who has been hurt by others' actions. We feel her pain to some extent. Let's take the next few minutes and unpack sweet Cindy's heart.

Let's open our Bibles to Psalm 51 and read it through once right now.

David writes this Psalm in two parts:
1. A deep heart of confession and a plea for pardon.
2. Worship in gratitude.

David cries out in verses 1–3, "Have mercy on me, O God according to your steadfast love according to your abundant mercy blot out my transgressions. Wash me thoroughly from my iniquity, and cleanse me from my sin! For I know my transgressions, and my sin is ever before me."

Contrast between David and Cindy:

Right off the top, we can see a wide contrast between Cindy's heart and David's. David acknowledges God, God's mercy, God's steadfast love, God's ability to restore, and his own desperate need for God's grace, and David takes full responsibility for his sin.

Cindy, on the other hand, is prideful, accusatory, critical, demeaning, and unforgiving, holds bitterness in her heart, and takes no responsibility for her sin.

Similarities between David and Cindy:

They both cry out, they are both broken, they both know God, and they are both sinners. But that's where the similarities stop.

David cries out to God, while Cindy cries out to the people in her life.
David says his brokenness is due to sin, while Cindy says her brokenness is due to others.
David worships God, while Cindy worships herself.
David hates his sin, while Cindy is blinded to her sin.

Look at David's understanding of his sin in Psalm 51:4: "Against you, you only, have I sinned and done what is evil in your sight, so that you may be justified in your words and blameless in your judgment."David had every right to be angry and bitter at others. He had been hurt by so many, he had been falsely accused and people were hunting him down to kill him. He had every human reason to be angry at God and his oppressors.

> David worships God, while Cindy worships herself.

But David also knew he was not perfect and had done things to hurt others as well. David humbly chose to acknowledge that he had sinned, but not only sinned, he sinned against God. David's humility was reflected in his ownership of his sin before a Holy God. He made no excuses, blamed no one else. He even said that his sin was evil before his God.

Defined By Your Past?

David used God as the standard for holiness. David saw his sin in contrast to God's holiness. A person with a prideful heart will always use his or her own life or other people's behavior as the standard. Let's look at a prideful heart using the list below.

> Pride is giving ourselves the credit for something that God has accomplished.
> Pride is taking the glory that belongs to God alone and keeping it for ourselves.
> Pride claims to be blameless.
> Pride will always blame shift.
> Pride minimizes our faults but maximizes those of others.
> Pride will make excuses.
> Pride is essentially self-worship.

"The fear of the Lord is hatred of evil. Pride and arrogance and the way of evil and perverted speech I hate" (Proverbs 8:13). Do we acknowledge our sins as evil done before a holy God? Do we measure ourselves against His righteousness? That is true humility.

Cindy's heart was full of pride, and she had little need for God. Her life was based on other people's actions and thoughts. She looked to others to find fulfillment, and when they did not deliver, she became angry and the root of bitterness dug deeper into her heart. Cindy was on the throne of her life, and she demanded to be worshipped.

Yes, Cindy was hurt by others throughout her life, as many of us have been. In some cases, those hurts were done by selfish, sinful people that cared little about the consequences and baggage they left behind.

God, more than anyone, sees that hurt, the pain, and the consequences. He loves you with unconditional love and wants to set you free from it all. God does not cause others to sin against you, but He can use those past experiences for good in your life.

> In Romans 6:1-14, Paul explains that if we have been united to Christ, we have also been united to him in his death and resurrection. We have died to sin and been raised to new life. This passage teaches that we have been freed from the power of sin, enabled to live in newness of life under the reign of grace, unified with Christ in his resurrection, and made new creatures. This passage emphasizes definitive sanctification, however Christians will always struggle against sin and continually be tempted by it this side of glory. According to 1 Corinthians 1:2, those who have been united to Christ have been sanctified, but there is still the reality that we will not be fully sanctified until glorification.[12]

Distinct Characteristics

Satan understands this truth and does not want you to be free. He wants to bring doubt to God's truth. He wants to accuse you with your past sins. He wants to define you by your past, he wants to tell you no one cares, no one loves you, and you're not valued, and he wants you to be very angry about it and trapped in a life of bitterness. Satan is a liar and wants to destroy you. He was deemed a murderer from the beginning and there is absolutely no truth in him. But, he is the great deceiver, and if we stray from God's truth, we are prone to believe his lies.

Bitterness is rooted in lies that we have chosen to believe.

Bitterness is rooted in lies that we have chosen to believe. Maybe you have realized for the first time that you might have bitterness, but, how do you know if you are trapped in bitterness? That's the problem. Bitterness is such a tricky sin. It is a tough sin to detect without the standard of God's Word. When we are not reading God's Word, it's hard to know what is real and what it is a lie.

What is bitterness? Why is it such a strong, gripping sin in our lives? Why can't we detect the bondage of bitterness in our hearts?

Bitterness is choosing unforgiveness.
Bitterness is selfish and prideful.
Bitterness is desiring revenge.

Paul writes, "Get rid of all bitterness, rage, anger, harsh words, and slander, as well as all types of malicious behavior. And be kind to one another, tenderhearted, forgiving one another, even as God in Christ forgave you" (Ephesians 4:31–32).

Bitterness comes with some friends. Rage, anger, harsh words, and slander, to name a few. Bitterness has very distinct characteristics. Look at the list below and see if any of these might be true in your own life:

Choosing not to forgive

Closing people out

Being disrespectful of others

Having a temper

Being critical of others

Blame-shifting

Being controlling

Being unthankful

Thinking everything is unfair

Replaying an offense over and over

Desiring to discredit others

Clenching your teeth when thinking of a certain person

Rejoicing in that person's hardships

Wishing bad on a person

Demanding rights

Demanding justice

Bitterness will always reflect a sinful heart of unforgiveness. When we choose to withhold forgiveness and harbor bitterness, we want to make our offender pay. We want to be the judge, jury, and sentencer. We want to decide the punishment that we feel is deserved. We, as the jury, declare our offender guilty and we, as the self-righteous judge, proclaim the sentencing on our offender. We lock him or her up and throw away the key, never to forgive that person.

> Bitterness is you drinking a glass of poison, hoping the other person dies.

"Therefore you have no excuse, O man, every one of you who judges. For in passing judgment on another you condemn yourself, because you, the judge, practice the very same things. We know that the judgment of God rightly falls on those who practice such things" (Romans 2:1–2).

God is clear. He is the only One who has the right to be the Judge. This verse tells us that when we pretend to be the judge we only reveal the sin in our own hearts. Bitterness will blind us to the truth. Bitterness will destroy us. Bitterness is you drinking a glass of poison, hoping the other person dies. Bitterness is a sin that affects everyone at some point. During all the years of counseling women, the number one root issue I deal with is bitterness. Cindy was one of those women. I picked up on her bitterness within the first few minutes of our first meeting. The clenched teeth, the squinting eyes, and the anger in her voice gave her away.

I used a little test on Cindy to help her gauge the depth of her bitter heart. I asked her, "Cindy, can you joyfully pray for God to bless (person's name) and rejoice with (person's name) when He does?"

Why don't you try that right now? Go through a list of names and see what stirs in your heart. Unfortunately, Cindy discovered that she was deep into bitterness. She knew she had turned away from God's truth, and that made it even easier for her to believe the enemy's lies.

If I...

If I choose to forgive this person, I will be letting him off the hook.

If I forgive this person, she will feel justified in her actions.

I can't trust God with this situation. He might go easy on him.

I need to make this person pay for what she did.

Do you find yourself thinking these thoughts? Satan has been spreading these gems for thousands of years. The bottom line is that these lies are rooted in a prideful, self-centered, self-focused, self-worshipping heart. We take our eyes off of God and place them on ourselves. We demand that others meet our expectations and when they don't, we are angry and bitter. We demand to get what we think we deserve.

When we push God out of our life, listen to the lies of the enemy, and demand to have our expectations met, we will never find peace. If we strive to get what we think we deserve, we will never be satisfied. What do we deserve? We deserve hell! That's the bottom line.

John Piper says it best:

> God in His great mercy delivered us from eternity in Hell and transferred us to eternity in Heaven through the redemption of Jesus Christ, the forgiveness of sins.[13]

We deserve hell and we are given heaven! "He has delivered us from the domain of darkness and transferred us to the kingdom of His beloved Son, in whom we have redemption, the forgiveness of sins" (Colossians 1:13–14).

> Make sure you see this most wonderful and astonishing of all truths: God took the record of your sins that made you destined to wrath (sins are offenses against God that bring down His wrath), and instead of holding them up in front of your face and using them as the warrant to send you to hell, He put them in the palm of His Son's hand and drove a nail through them into the cross."[14]

Like David, we must see our great need for God. We must be reminded of the incredible forgiveness that we have been given. The forgiveness we do not deserve.

Standard for Life

We need to have gratitude for God, through Jesus Christ, who graciously and mercifully forgave ALL of our wicked, evil sins. Not just some, but ALL.

David understood this and he cried out for mercy. He saw his sin as wretched and evil. He saw God's holiness and righteousness as the standard for his life. Do we?

"The aim of confession [of sin] then is not to erase consequences, it's to restore joy. And then the consequences are what they are. Your sins have consequences. They're rocks thrown in the pond and the ripples go and they touch every shore. But God does promise when you've confessed and repented that He will show you lovingkindness and compassion because you are His eternal child...

> "The aim of confession [of sin] then is not to erase consequences, it's to restore joy."

Your justification is settled forever. Don't cover your sin, confess it. That's what true Christians do. You've been bathed that you need continually to have your feet washed as they get dirty walking in your fallenness. If you don't confess, you'll be chastened. If you do confess, you may never be able to change the consequences but because you're God's child He'll come to you in compassion and lovingkindness and minister to you."[15]

There is a happy ending to Cindy's story. After an entire year of weekly meetings together, I had the privilege of walking Cindy through the pages of Scripture as God graciously showed her His loving mercy and forgiveness. Her eyes were opened to the root sin of bitterness in heart. She became aware of the sins that she harbored against God. Through it all, she chose to repent, surrender, be forgiven and restored into an intimate fellowship with her Father, and joyfully walk in His truth.

Cindy chose to put off "bitterness and wrath and anger and clamor and slander . . . along with all malice."

Gracious Forgiveness

Cindy chose to "be kind . . . tenderhearted, forgiving . . . as God in Christ forgave [her]" (Ephesians 4:31–32).

Cindy chose to put off the bitterness and put on forgiveness. She made a conscience effort to go before each family member, as well as others, asking forgiveness for the sin she had committed against God and them. She chose to be very detailed in her confession, not wanting to leave any room for the enemy to have the slightest bit of ground.

Graciously, each one chose to forgive her. She humbly accepted and joyfully received their gracious forgiveness. That brought great unity, joy, and peace into her family. Her life now reflects kindness, tenderheartedness, and grace. Not everything is perfect in her life, but no matter the circumstance, Cindy has learned to choose joy in all things.

Reflection:

Steps to Freedom from Bitterness

Set aside a few hours and follow these steps one by one.

It is a great tool to walk you to freedom over bitterness.

Use your Companion Journal to do the following:

1. Make a list of how a certain person or persons has offended you.

2. Make a list of your sins that have caused offenses in others' lives.

3. Make a list of things you've done for which God has forgiven you.

4. Ask God to help you view the person or persons who has wronged you as a tool in His hand.

5. Ask God to forgive you for your bitterness toward the person or persons.

6. Decide in your heart to assume total responsibility for your sin.

7. If you feel it's appropriate and will not cause more problems than it solves, go to that person, confess the bitterness you have unjustly held against him or her, and ask that person for his or her forgiveness. Remember, you are assuming responsibility for your sin; you are not trying to solicit a confession from this person.

In closing, we have two choices: We can allow bitterness to destroy us, or we can allow God to develop us into the people He wants us to be. We must choose to view our circumstances as tools God uses to further develop our spiritual lives.

Prayer:

> Father, thank You for the mercy You've graciously shown me. Please give me the ability to forgive those who have wronged me. I want to be completely free from bitterness and its devastating consequences. In Jesus's name, I pray. Amen.[16]

Day 2 - Bitterness

✱ Make sure to have your Bible, Companion Journal, and pen.

✱ Pray before you start. Use the guided prayer.

✱ Open your Bible and read the Scripture selected for today.

✱ Begin learning your Scripture memory verse and review it throughout the week.

Prayer: Use this prayer as a guide.

> *Dear merciful, gracious Father, I come to You undeservedly and am humbled by Your continued unconditional love. Your mercies are new every morning. They never end. Oh God, I cry out to You like David, "Have mercy on me, O God, Have mercy on me, O God, according to your steadfast love; according to your abundant mercy, blot out my transgressions. Wash me thoroughly from my iniquity, and cleanse me from my sin!"*

Recite your Scripture Memory - Psalm 51:1, 2.

"Have mercy on me, O God, according to Your steadfast love;
according to Your abundant mercy blot out my transgressions.
Wash me thoroughly from my iniquity, and cleanse me from my sin!"

Open your Bible to Psalm 51. Read the entire chapter once.

Day 2 Questions - Use your Companion Journal to answer the questions.

1. What does the word "mercy" mean to you?

2. What does God's steadfast love mean to you?

3. What truths do you see in Psalm 51: 4?

4. Describe David's heart in your own words.

Meditate on Psalm 51:1, 2.

"Have mercy on me, O God, according to your steadfast love; according to your abundant mercy blot out my transgressions. Wash me thoroughly from my iniquity, and cleanse me from my sin!"

Close this time in grateful worship and prayer.

Day 3 - Bitterness

* Make sure to have your Bible, Companion Journal, and pen.

* Pray before you start. Use the guided prayer.

* Open your Bible and read the Scripture selected for today.

* Begin learning your Scripture memory verse and review it throughout the week.

Prayer: Use this prayer as a guide.

> *Dear Father, I humbly come asking You to give me a heart that desires You above all else. I know that You are the only one who can bring contentment, joy, and peace into my life. I praise You because You are worthy of honor and glory. You are the Holy One of my life and I want to be cleaned of my ongoing bondage to sin, so I may reflect Your grace and mercy to others. Through the blood and name of Jesus Christ my Redeemer, Amen.*

Recite your Scripture Memory - Psalm 51:1, 2.

"Have mercy on me, O God, according to Your steadfast love;
according to Your abundant mercy blot out my transgressions.
Wash me thoroughly from my iniquity, and cleanse me from my sin!"

Open your Bible to Psalm 51. Read the entire chapter once.

Day 3 Questions - Use your Companion Journal to answer the questions.

1. According to Psalm 51: 1 - 2, how does David say his transgressions will be blotted out?

2. Why is it important to acknowledge that our sin is against God?

3. Of the following, which words do you most relate to and why?
- Anger
- Worry
- Bitterness
- Fear
- Doubt
- Gossip
- Critical Spirt

4. Whom do you feel bitter toward and why?

Meditate on Psalm 51:3, 4.

"For I know my transgressions, and my sin is ever before me. Against you, you only, have I sinned and done what is evil in your sight, so that you may be justified in your words and blameless in your judgment."

Close this time in grateful worship and prayer.

Day 4 - Bitterness

* Make sure to have your Bible, Companion Journal, and pen.
* Pray before you start. Use the guided prayer.
* Open your Bible and read the Scripture reading for today.
* Begin learning your Scripture memory verse and review it throughout the week.

Prayer: Use this prayer as a guide.

> *Dear Father, I humbly come before You with a surrendered heart. You are worthy of all my praise and adoration. Help me to forgive others as You have forgiven me. Your forgiveness and reconciliation are a huge blessing in my life. Father, help me to see You in all grace and mercy. I am grateful that You show me such kindness. I surrender this time to You. In Jesus's holy name, Amen.*

Recite your Scripture Memory - Psalm 51:1, 2.

"Have mercy on me, O God, according to Your steadfast love;
according to Your abundant mercy blot out my transgressions.
Wash me thoroughly from my iniquity, and cleanse me from my sin!"

Open your Bible to Psalm 51. Read the entire chapter once.

Day 4 Questions - Use your Companion Journal to answer the questions.

1. What is the opposite of bitterness?

2. Why is it hard to give up the sin of bitterness?

3. Pride is essentially self-worship. Describe what this means to you.

4. Would you be willing to ask God to bless the person you are most struggling to forgive? Why or why not?

Meditate on Psalm 51:10 – 12.

"Create in me a clean heart, O God, and renew a right spirit within me. Cast me not away from your presence, and take not your Holy Spirit from me. Restore to me the joy of your salvation, and uphold me with a willing spirit."

Close this time in grateful worship and prayer.

Day 5 - Bitterness

* Make sure to have your Bible, Companion Journal, and pen.
* Pray before you start. Use the guided prayer.
* Open your Bible and read the Scripture selected for today.
* Begin learning your Scripture memory verse and review it throughout the week.

Prayer: Use this prayer as a guide.

> *Dear almighty God, my God, "O Lord, open my lips, and my mouth will declare Your praise." I want to speak of Your magnificence to all who will listen. Help me to show love and kindness to my loved ones. Help me not be critical, but show Your mercy and grace instead. You are worthy of my surrendered heart. May I continually want to have a clean heart before You! In the sweet name of Jesus, Amen.*

Recite your Scripture Memory - Psalm 51:1, 2.

"Have mercy on me, O God, according to Your steadfast love;
according to Your abundant mercy blot out my transgressions.
Wash me thoroughly from my iniquity, and cleanse me from my sin!"

Open your Bible to Psalm 51. Read the entire chapter once.

Day 5 Questions - Use your Companion Journal to answer the questions.

1. Why do a critical spirit, anger, and bitterness seem to work together so well?

2. Why does Jesus tell His disciples to forgive seven times seventy a day?

3. How long have you been in bondage to bitterness and how long will you choose to stay here? What must you do to get rid of bitterness?

4. God tells us we must ask God for forgiveness for our sin of bitterness and we must ask forgiveness from those toward whom we held bitterness. Who will you ask forgiveness from? Make a list and surrender these people to God. Then go to the individuals and ask their forgiveness.

Meditate on Colossians 1:13 – 14.

"He has delivered us from the domain of darkness and transferred us to the kingdom of his beloved Son, in whom we have redemption, the forgiveness of sins."

Remember, in His great mercy, we deserve hell but we receive heaven!

Close this time in grateful worship and prayer.

Day 6 - The Good Portion - A Time of Worship

This is the day of the week that you do as Mary did and sit for an extended amount of time in prayer and worship. Block out at least an hour, perhaps more, once a week, to have extended time to be still, sit quietly all by yourself, and simply worship your Father.

Use Psalm 51 to guide your praise for God.

1. Praise (Use Psalm 51 to guide you).

2. Gratitude (Use Psalm 51 to guide you).

3. Worship (Sing).

4. Recite one of your Scriptures back to God from memory. Hiding God's Word in your heart is a beautiful way to show God that you value Him and His thoughts.

5. Like David, cry out with the sin of bitterness and those you have held bitterness toward in your heart. Confess, repent, and ask for forgivingness.

6. Pray and ask God to help you value eternal things and to give you a heart of worship like Mary's (see Luke 10).

7. Close this time in prayer.
(ACTS - Adoration, Confession, Thanksgiving, and Supplication).

7
Anger

7 Anger

Chapter 7 - Anger

Day 1

* Make sure to have your Bible, Companion Journal, and pen.
* Pray before you start.
* Open your Bible and read the Scripture reading for today
* Read Chapter 7 of <u>The Good Portion.</u>
* Begin learning your Scripture memory verse so you will be ready to recite it on Day 6.

Daily Scripture Reading - Galatians 5

Scripture memory - Galatians 5:22 – 24.

"But the fruit of the Spirit is love, joy, peace, patience, kindness, goodness, faithfulness, gentleness, self-control; against such things there is no law. And those who belong to Christ Jesus have crucified the flesh with its passions and desires."

Chapter 7

Years ago, Sandra contacted me asking if we could meet. She needed help with a tough situation and it seemed urgent. She sounded desperate and she anxiously pushed me to meet as soon as possible. My schedule was very full that week, but I was able to squeeze her in around lunchtime one afternoon. I'd like Sandra to share her story with you.

Sandra' Story

My name is Sandra. I contacted Heidi and asked if we could meet. I was at the end of my rope. I felt utterly hopeless in my role as a mom and a wife. I have five children and have been married for eighteen years. I am a Christian and am involved in my church regularly. Before I met with Heidi, I would have said my relationship with God, my husband, and my children was fairly good, not great, just as good as could be expected under the circumstances. I asked Heidi to meet with me to see if she could give me some advice on parenting my strong-willed, angry, seemingly defiant ten-year-old daughter.

After a few meetings with Heidi, she began to point me in a direction I had not intended to go. I had no interest in a conversation about what she wanted to talk about. I came to her to receive some parenting tips on how to fix this angry daughter of mine and I felt like Heidi had a different plan.

All I needed from Heidi was a few practical tips to ease the situation at home. I was desperate for help with my daughter. I'd tried everything. I'd punished her, I'd grounded her, I'd taken away all her media devices, lectured her, yelled, threatened, even ignored her at times, and prayed a lot.

I began to understand that my relationship with God was marred by bitterness, shame, guilt, and fear.

My daughter was disrupting our home, and things had to change. I was a mess, my marriage was suffering, and no one was happy. I found myself so mad at God for giving me this rude, disrespectful, angry daughter and a husband who didn't seem to care about anything. I did not ask for this life.

It seemed as though whatever I said or did angered my daughter. I was trying to be a good parent, but she brought out the ugliness in me. I won't lie and tell you I acted like a loving, godly mother all the time. Sure, I got angry, I yelled, I criticized, I threatened, and I did what every mom does—I cried a lot.

Heidi did give me some helpful tips on keeping peace in the home for the time being, but it seemed like our conversations revolved around me a lot, not my daughter. I couldn't understand why at first, but the reason soon became very clear.

Over the weeks, Heidi gently helped me see, through God's Word and a nudge from the Holy Spirit, that I, too, like my daughter, was a strong-willed, angry, seemingly defiant daughter to my heavenly Father. This was something I had never realized before. It was something I didn't want to see, but it was sadly and painfully true. I was a very angry, controlling woman.

I began to understand that my relationship with God was marred by bitterness, shame, guilt, and fear. I was angry at God, my husband, my children, and my past relationships. I blame-shifted all my frustrations, discontentment, and lack of joy onto the closest people in my life. I was mad at God for my past. I was mad at God for the family He gave me. I was one angry woman.

Wrong Expectations

The emotional neglect I felt as a child was heartbreaking to me, and I had never forgiven my parents for it. My parents had asked for my forgiveness many times, but I refused them the satisfaction. I would punish them by withholding my forgiveness. Bitterness had taken root.

Heidi helped me see that my expectations were in the wrong places. I was expecting the people in my life to fix and fulfill what only God could do. I placed undue pressure on my family and friends to fill a void that they could never succeed in filling. Their failure to meet my expectations made me feel like everyone was failing me. I felt trapped and hopeless in a life that had no joy and was filled with outbursts of anger, criticism, and blame-shifting.

Often, I would think, "If only others around me would behave properly, then I would be happy. If only my children would just obey, then I would be a joyful mom. If my husband would only treat me better, then I would be a more loving wife."

"If only ..." These were my thoughts every day of my life. Every day was a failure in my mind because I was so unhappy and it was "their" fault, which led me to feel so discouraged. My circumstances seemed so hopeless.

I carried unresolved bitterness into my adulthood, into my marriage, and into all of my relationships. The result of all these unresolved issues was a welling up of a heart of anger at everyone and every circumstance I didn't like.

Sandra's story is similar to those of many of the women I counsel. These women feel trapped in a marriage, family, or life they wish they could change. They have the beautiful picture in their heads of what their life should look like and one they feel they rightly deserve. But unfortunately, the people in their lives have robbed them of realizing these expectations, and their well-deserved, picturesque life never comes about. Instead, anger abounds.

Waging a War in Us

So, why are we so prone to anger? Why is it so easy to lose control and lash out with ugly, hurtful words? We hate that we let loose, but it just happens. Let's see what Paul has to say about this in Galatians.

Open your Bibles to Galatians 5:1. Paul tells us, "For freedom Christ has set us free; stand firm therefore, and do not submit again to a yoke of slavery." He tells us not to submit to the yoke of sin, like anger, and be enslaved by it. We have already been set free, so why do we choose to place ourselves under the bondage of sin?

Anger is one of those sins that can take root in our hearts, as in Sandra's, and rule us. We can be imprisoned by the root of anger, and Paul asks us why we would choose that over living in freedom.

So, what, exactly, is anger?

> Sinful anger is a selfish response to not getting what I want. We become sinfully angry because our pleasures (desires which are not necessarily sinful in and of themselves, such as the desire for our spouses to respect us or our children to obey us) have become so intense that they are waging war within our members. When our desires (as good as they may be) become so strong that they wage a military campaign in our hearts, otherwise lawful desires become sinful, idolatrous desires—not because they are sinful desires per se but because they are desired inordinately. Our hearts covet them so intensely that we are willing to sin (to go to war and fight) either in order to obtain our desires or because we are not able to obtain them.[17]

> Sinful anger is sort of like God's built-in smoke detector—it lets us
> know that we are coveting something to the point of idolatry.[18]

Sandra blew up because of the anger in her heart. Anger demanded that someone must fulfill the idols of her heart.

- ✦ Anger demands that you give me what I want.
- ✦ Anger demands that I must have it now.
- ✦ Anger demands that I will not let anyone stand in my way of getting what I want.
- ✦ Anger demands that you are robbing me of what I think I deserve.

Anger is fueled by idolatry. It is demanding and selfish and will destroy relationships. John Piper explains, "Most of our bitterness and anger towards others is rooted in an inability to be profoundly amazed at Christ's love for us in our sin. If you are struggling with bitterness then it may be that the Lord is letting the very sin that is flowing from your inability to see Christ be the means by which you come to see him. In other words, perhaps this season of rage, anger, and a fed-up "I'm out of here and don't want anything to do with you" spirit is where you have had to come in order to see the greatness of your sin as a forgiven and justified saint. And the Lord has done it so that you would be stunned at his grace in a deeper way than you've ever been stunned by the grace of God before. And now, out of that experience can flow grace towards others." [19]

> Anger is fueled by idolatry. It is demanding and selfish and will destroy relationships.

Her Perceived Rights

All of Sandra's relationships were being destroyed because of sin. Sandra was unhappy and demanded that the people in her life make her happy. Every day that they did not fulfill her exceptions, she grew deeper into bitterness and anger. This was exposed in three areas.

Sandra's sin of **bitterness**: she refused to forgive those who robbed her of her perceived rights.

Sandra's sin of **idolatry**: she demanded that the desires of her heart be fulfilled.

Sandra's sin of **anger**: if she couldn't have her desires, she would demand through yelling, seething, or venting.

Damaging Culprit in Relationships

"Let all bitterness and wrath and anger and clamor and slander be put away from you, along with all malice" (Ephesians 4:31).

Again, God is telling us to put these things away from us and He gave us the power through Jesus Christ to accomplish this. Look at Galatians 5:13–15 in your Bible. Paul tells us that we can be free from the bondage of sin and the sin of anger, and to use that freedom to serve others. There are two truths here. Sin is always used to serve self, and freedom in Christ is used to serve others.

Sandra began to learn this lesson and will share a bit of how God slowly opened her heart to the truth of the bondage to the sin she was holding onto. Listen to what she says.

> God's kind grace opened my eyes to see that the lack of joy and peace, which I so desperately wanted and could never seem to achieve, was due to the weight of unconfessed sin in my life and the idols of my heart with which I had replaced God. Now, there was nothing wrong with my desire to have peace, joy, and contentment. That is a good thing, but I was looking for people to fulfill what only God could give me. It was selfish on my part to demand that others fulfill these desires. It was a no-win situation. I put undue pressure on them to give me the desires of my heart, and when they did not do what I demanded they do, I was angry at them for robbing me of what I desired. God mercifully showed me the wicked idolatry of my heart.

Are you feeling the weight of Sandra's story? She came to me because her daughter was "out of control" and Sandra just wanted to fix her. But, by God's grace, He showed Sandra that her daughter was just reflecting her.

Scripture teaches us that anger is a damaging culprit in many relationships. Anger displays our lack of grace, our self-centeredness, and our "me"-focused demands.

"A man of wrath stirs up strife, and one given to anger causes much transgression" (Proverbs 29:22).

We are the first to complain when our lives are full of strife, arguing, disunity, and disrespect. We don't like it and we point fingers at everyone else, demanding that they fix it. We declare in our minds ,and out loud, that the other person is to blame for the mess. But God says that we must evaluate our hearts to see if we are not the ones being divisive, controlling, demanding, sulking, and argumentative.

Look at Galatians 5:16–18. Paul speaks to this very problem. He says we are always fighting the sins of the flesh. He shows us how the spirit and the flesh are opposed to one another. The Holy Spirit will always fight for God's righteousness to be evident in our lives, and our flesh will fight for sin to abound and reveal itself through us.

It's easy to point fingers at others, but we must first examine our hearts to see if we have idols that have replaced God in our hearts. Look at the lists below and see

Blow up responses

how you might be displaying your anger:
- ☐ Yelling/screaming
- ☐ Throwing
- ☐ Kicking/hitting
- ☐ Talking back
- ☐ Quarreling
- ☐ Using biting sarcasm
- ☐ Name-calling
- ☐ Using profanity
- ☐ Using contemptuous speech
- ☐ Saying hurtful things you later regret

Clam up responses

- ☐ Sulking
- ☐ Pouting
- ☐ Crying
- ☐ Giving "the silent treatment"
- ☐ Giving the "cold shoulder"
- ☐ Withdrawing/retreating
- ☐ Refusing to talk
- ☐ Going for a walk or drive [20]

We are prone to express anger in two ways, blowing up or clamming up. God says all anger is sinful because we are demanding something we think we can't live without and if we don't get it, we are angry. God calls that idolatry. We desire something more than God.

"You shall have no other gods before Me" (Exodus 20:3–6). This is the first of the Ten Commandments!

> God does speak of righteous anger. Righteous anger is motivated by Godward and biblically-informed concerns. Before it sees how someone has offended me, it sees how he has offended God. My child has not embarrassed me with his display of rudeness, he has violated God's command to honor father and mother. Jones says it well: Righteous anger throbs with kingdom concerns.

> Finally, righteous anger is accompanied by other godly qualities and expresses itself in godly ways. True anger properly diagnoses what is actual sin, it focuses not on personal offense as much as Godward offense, and then it expresses itself in ways consistent with Christian character.[21]

Who makes you angry?

The answer is that YOU make YOU angry. No one can MAKE you angry. You are the cause of your own anger. Now I know that sounds harsh, but the reality is, we choose to be angry. We choose to demand that others fulfill the desires of our idolatrous hearts. And when they don't, we react sinfully. This type of anger is a sin!

Anger is unpredictable and can erupt without warning. If this is a habit and happens often, without warning, I would say that person has the root issue of anger in his or her heart. Explosive anger is much easier to detect.

Think about it … have you been to a basketball, hockey, or baseball game where a fight breaks out? What usually starts it? Someone feels like their perceived rights have been violated and it stirs the anger in their heart and they go on the attack, seemingly without any control. Anything that controls us outside of God is sin and an idol of our heart.

God knows when we choose to allow anger to take root in our hearts, we can never produce the righteousness of God. We can't harbor sin and reflect God's character at the same time. "For the anger of man does not produce the righteousness of God" (James 1:20).

We can put on the facade of God's character for a time, but if we are choosing to live in sin, we will eventually reflect what is truly in our hearts. How we react in stressful situations will always reveal our true character. Making God the idol of our hearts is the only way we can ever produce good fruit and reflect His character.

The answer to having freedom over sinful anger:

1. Confess, repent, and ask God for His forgiveness.
2. Replace anger with God's love, joy, peace, patience, kindness, goodness, faithfulness, gentleness, and self-control.

> When a sinner is truly repentant and comes to God in a broken and contrite spirit and asks for forgiveness and God forgives and transforms, it is the working of the Holy Spirit.[22]

We must choose obedience and the Holy Spirit will convict, strengthen, and encourage our hearts to continue through to victory in Christ Jesus! "For freedom Christ has set us free; stand firm therefore" (Galatians 5:1).

God has already set you free through His Son, Jesus. Stand firm, child of God, and live in that freedom.

Reflection:

◆ Stop and pray right now and ask God to graciously and kindly reveal any anger to which you may be in bondage.

◆ Write out a list of the idols you are holding onto that you can see lead to a root of anger.

◆ One by one, acknowledge these idols to God. Humbly confess these to God. Then ask for His gracious forgiveness for each one. Humbly ask God to forgive you for choosing to worship another god. I John 1: 9 tells us He promises to forgive us immediately when we ask.

◆ You can be free from the bondage of anger right now through the power of God in Christ Jesus. Freedom in Christ is graciously offered to you this very moment. Whom will you choose to worship?

◆ Write out a prayer to God thanking Him for the freedom you are so graciously given in Christ.

Day 2 - Anger

* Make sure to have your Bible, Companion Journal, and pen.
* Pray before you start. Use the guided prayer.
* Open your Bible and read the Scripture selected for today.
* Begin learning your Scripture memory verse and review it throughout the week.

Prayer: Use this prayer as a guide.

> *God, holy, just, righteous God, I humbly come to You with a humble heart. I know that You desire me and call me Your child. That brings me such joy. Through Your Son, Jesus, I am redeemed and reconciled to You. Thank You for sacrificing Your one and only Son on my behalf. Open my eyes to Your truth right now. In Jesus's name, Amen.*

Recite your Scripture memory - Galatians 5:22 – 24.

"But the fruit of the Spirit is love, joy, peace, patience, kindness, goodness, faithfulness, gentleness, self-control; against such things there is no law. And those who belong to Christ Jesus have crucified the flesh with its passions and desires."

Open your Bible to Galatians 5. Read the entire chapter one time through.

Day 2 Questions - Use your Companion Journal to answer the questions.

1. Read Galatians 5: 1. What did Christ do and what are we to do?

2. "For freedom, Christ has set us free." Christ's will for you is that you enjoy freedom. Freedom from what?

3. What does Paul say about the yoke of slavery in verse 1? How does that relate to you?

4. When we embrace the law as our rule of walking with God, we must let go of Jesus. He is no longer our righteousness; we attempt to earn it ourselves (see Galatians 5: 2-4). Describe what this means in your own words.

Meditate on Galatians 5:1.

"For freedom Christ has set us free; stand firm therefore, and do not submit again to a yoke of slavery."

Close this time in grateful worship and prayer.

Day 3 - Anger

✱ Make sure to have your Bible, Companion Journal, and pen.

✱ Pray before you start. Use the guided prayer.

✱ Open your Bible and read the Scripture reading for today.

✱ Begin learning your Scripture memory verse and review it throughout the week.

Prayer: Use this prayer as a guide.

> *Dear gracious Abba Father, You are my God. I acknowledge you are my Daddy. I love Your name. I ask You to quiet my heart and allow me to sense Your presence. Let Your Holy Spirit open my eyes to Your Word right now. I lift Your name on high and praise You, in the name of Jesus, Amen.*

Recite your Scripture Memory - Galatians 5:22 – 24.

"But the fruit of the Spirit is love, joy, peace, patience, kindness, goodness, faithfulness, gentleness, self-control; against such things there is no law. And those who belong to Christ Jesus have crucified the flesh with its passions and desires."

Open your Bible to Galatians 5. Read the entire chapter one time through.

Day 3 Questions - Use your Companion Journal to answer the questions.

1. Look at Galatians 5: 7. How are we like a running well?

2. Paul speaks of the false teaching that was in the church (see Galatians 5: 8, 9). How have you allowed lies to creep into your own life?

3. Describe how you are were called to freedom (see Galatians 5: 13).

4. How does Paul warn us to use our freedoms in Christ (see Galatians 5: 13)?

Meditate on Galatians 5:13 – 14.

"For you were called to freedom, brothers. Only do not use your freedom as an opportunity for the flesh, but through love serve one another. For the whole law is fulfilled in one word: You shall love your neighbor as yourself."

Close this time in grateful worship and prayer.

Day 4 - Anger

✱ Make sure to have your Bible, Companion Journal, and pen.

✱ Pray before you start. Use the guided prayer.

✱ Open your Bible and read the Scripture reading for today.

✱ Begin learning your Scripture memory verse and review it throughout the week.

Prayer: Use this prayer as a guide.

> *Dear Yahweh, my God, Who is always there, I bow in humble adoration to You, Almighty, risen King, You will never leave me or forsake me. I praise You for choosing me and allowing me the privilege of knowing You. In Jesus' Holy Name, Amen.*

Recite your Scripture Memory - Galatians 5:22 – 24.

"But the fruit of the Spirit is love, joy, peace, patience, kindness, goodness, faithfulness, gentleness, self-control; against such things there is no law. And those who belong to Christ Jesus have crucified the flesh with its passions and desires."

Open your Bible to Galatians 5. Read the entire chapter one time through.

Day 4 Questions - Use your Companion Journal to answer the questions.

1. "But if you bite and devour one another, watch out that you are not consumed by one another" (see Galatians 5: 15). How do you see this happening in your home?

2. Why should we submit ourselves to God to avoid anger?

3. What are the signs you see in yourself that point to your possible angry heart?

4. What does Galatians 5: 17 tell us about the importance of the Spirit and the flesh?

Meditate on Galatians 5:17.

"For the desires of the flesh are against the Spirit, and the desires of the Spirit are against the flesh, for these are opposed to each other, to keep you from doing the things you want to do."

Close this time in grateful worship and prayer.

Day 5 - Anger

* Make sure to have your Bible, Companion Journal, and pen.

* Pray before you start. Use the guided prayer.

* Open your Bible and read the Scripture selected for today.

* Begin learning your Scripture memory verse and review it throughout the week.

Prayer: Use this prayer as a guide.

> *Dear Father God, I cry out to You because my heart needs You. I am desperate for Your grace and mercy. I long for Your Word to penetrate my heart and give me a renewed mind. Thank You for being gracious to me. I praise You for giving me the Holy Spirit. In the name of my Savior, Jesus Christ, Amen.*

Recite your Scripture Memory - Galatians 5:22 – 24.

"But the fruit of the Spirit is love, joy, peace, patience, kindness, goodness, faithfulness, gentleness, self-control; against such things there is no law. And those who belong to Christ Jesus have crucified the flesh with its passions and desires."

Open your Bible to Galatians 5. Read the entire chapter one time through.

Day 5 Questions - Use your Companion Journal to answer the questions.

1. What is the opposite of pride? Answer and then define.

2. What are we to put off in Galatians 5: 19-21?

3. What are we to put on in Galatians 5: 22-23?

4. Describe what this means to you: "Those who belong to Christ Jesus have crucified the flesh with its passions and desires" (see Galatians 5: 24).

5. What does Paul warn us to do and not do in Galatians 5: 25-26?

Meditate on Galatians 5:22 – 24.

"But the fruit of the Spirit is love, joy, peace, patience, kindness, goodness, faithfulness, gentleness, self-control; against such things there is no law. And those who belong to Christ Jesus have crucified the flesh with its passions and desires."

Close this time in grateful worship and prayer.

Day 6 - The Good Portion - A Time of Worship

This is the day of the week that you do as Mary did and sit for an extended amount of time in prayer and worship. Block out at least an hour, perhaps more, once a week, to have extended time to be still, sit quietly all by yourself, and simply worship your Father.

Use Galatians 5 to guide your praise for God.

1. Praise (Use Galatians 5 to guide you).

2. Gratitude (Use Galatians 5 to guide you).

3. Worship (Sing).

4. Cry out to God with the lies you are believing and ask His forgiveness.

5. Pray
(ACTS - Adoration, Confession, Thanksgiving, and Supplication).

6. Recite one of your Scriptures back to God from memory. Hiding God's Word in your heart is a beautiful way to show God that you value Him and His thoughts.

7. Write out a closing prayer committing to believing God's truth.

8

Put Off-Put On

8 Put Off - Put On

Chapter 8 - Put Off / Put On

Day 1

* Make sure to have your Bible, Companion Journal, and pen.
* Pray before you start.
* Open your Bible and read the Scripture reading for today.
* Read Chapter 8 of <u>The Good Portion</u>.
* Begin learning your Scripture memory verse so you will be ready to recite it on Day 6.

Daily Scripture Reading - Psalm 119

Scripture Memory - Psalm 119:127 – 128.

"Therefore I love your commandments above gold, above fine gold. Therefore I consider all your precepts to be right; I hate every false way."

Chapter 8

I was eight and a half months pregnant, anticipating the day our sweet baby, number nine, would be born. In just a couple of weeks, we would finally hold our little munchkin for the first time. We were well prepared for another home birth. The casseroles were all made, diapers were bought, the infant car seat was dusted off, the bassinet was assembled, blankets and sheets were thoroughly sterilized, and now all

Mike and I Began to Cry

we had to do was just wait for the big day.

I'll be honest, I did have a slight concern that our little one was not as active as I was used to. He or she did not seem to move much. I didn't want to say anything, because I figured it was just my protective mama side coming out. But it was beginning to consume my thoughts, so I mentioned this to my midwife on one of my weekly appointments. She could see my concerned, worried look and offered to run a few tests, listen to the baby's heartbeat, and hopefully bring some relief to my anxious mind.

As she moved the doppler around my huge belly, she seemed to be struggling to find the heartbeat, which made me a bit nervous. I intentionally stared at her face to see just how concerned she became. Soon, she found the heartbeat, but I could tell by her expression that there was something amiss. She said, "Let's go to the doctor and get a sonogram, just to ease your mind."

My husband, Mike, immediately left work and met us at the doctors' office. We were called into the examining room almost immediately and a kind older gentleman entered with a nurse in tow. The doctor introduced himself and gently shook our hands. He reminded me of my kind grandpa, just a little younger.

First, they ran blood work, then the doctor began the slow, long, tedious process of the ultrasound. He methodically and quietly studied the screen, not saying a word, and seemed to take forever. I zeroed in on his every expression, looking for clues of concern, worry, or possibly a welcoming smile.

After what seemed like hours, he turned the machine off and sat still for a moment as he gathered his thoughts and then looked at us with the most grandfatherly, tender look and said, "Well, there is a problem, and sadly none of the scenarios are very good. But, first, do you want to know the gender?" My husband and I looked at each other and agreed that we would like to know. He said, "It's a boy." Mike and I began to cry. This was our Matthew Paul. We felt even more connected to our little guy but knew the next bit of information we were about to receive would change our lives forever.

This Happens to Other People

Music to Our Ears

The kind, gentle doctor spoke quietly as he informed us of the three possible diagnoses. Matthew would have one of the following; Down syndrome, trisomy 13, or trisomy 18. He explained that Down syndrome is viable for a healthy long life, with limitations, of course, but, sadly, trisomy 13 and 18 are both usually fatal, if not right away, within the first year. He said we wouldn't know the results of the diagnosis until after Matthew was born. The doctor left us alone to ponder the news. My first thought was, "This happens to other people, not us." I then wondered what this news meant for our lives, our emotions, and our eight children, who would face this trial with us.

We drove home in tears after the doctor appointment, opened the front door, and were greeted by our precious children. They were eagerly waiting to hear the results of the tests. I burst into tears as soon as I saw all of their sweet, curious little faces. My three-year-old, Suzanna, clung to my legs. Mike had the tough job of explaining what the future looked like for our family. Things were going to be very different, and none of us would ever be the same, no matter what happened from this day forward.

> We drove home in tears after the doctor appointment...

Too quickly, the day came and I was admitted into the hospital for a scheduled C-section. The night before my 5:00 a.m. delivery, alone with my sweet husband, we began to cry out to the Lord for His mercy and comfort. It was one of the longest, hardest, and sweetest nights of our lives. We immersed ourselves in His Word, especially the Psalms.

In Psalm 119:48–50, David cries out to God, "I will lift up my hands toward your commandments, which I love, and I will meditate on your statutes. Remember your word to your servant, in which you have made me hope. This is my comfort in my affliction, that your promise gives me life."

Like David, we found great peace in God's Word, and our hearts were comforted by the Holy Spirit. The enemy tried to bring doubt and fear, but we put off the lies and clung to the powerful, steadfast truth of God's Word.

Five o'clock finally came and I was wheeled into the operating room, where I was prepped for my C-section. Soon, we would meet our precious little Matthew Paul. The truth of his condition was about to be revealed. We had no idea if he would live for one minute, one hour, one day, or years. There were many nurses on hand, standing in ready anticipation to whisk our little guy away to the NICU.

Like most expectant parents, we longed to hear the precious cry of our sweet little baby boy. The moment finally came. Would he make it through the birth? Would he live for an hour? Would he survive a day? So many unknowns lay before us, but all our questions were about to be answered.

Everyone was in place and ready to go. Then we heard the doctor say, "He's here." Matthew was safely delivered, but we didn't hear him cry. I held my breath and then I heard the most beautiful sound these mama's ears could have ever imagined. He cried. He was alive. His little cry was like sweet music that took away every fear at that moment. It brought tears to our eyes. Our baby was alive. We were so grateful to God our Matthew had made it this far.

It seemed as though everyone was in emergency mode. They briefly showed Matthew to me as they wrapped him up and hurriedly took him to the NICU. Since I was not able to go, Mike followed the nurses to the emergency room. We just didn't know how long he would live, and Mike wanted to be the one holding his little hand if he should take his last breath on earth.

After recovery, I was taken to my room. I was informed that the hospital waiting room was packed with many loving family and sweet friends praying and singing hymns. God was being glorified!

As I patiently yearned to hold my baby, Mike finally came into the room, smiled, and said, "Our Matthew is beautiful and breathing, but he needs a few more tests." Mike seemed cautious not to say any more than that.

Soon, the doctors arrived, and I intensely studied their faces to see if I could figure out the diagnosis, possibly as a way to prepare my emotions for what they were about to present to us. The doctors first gave us the medical overview of chromosomal issues in babies. Most of that went over my head and I was honestly just listening for the one word I dreaded—trisomy. After what seemed like an eternity, they finally gave us the dreaded news. They gently said, "Your baby has trisomy 18 and has only a few hours to live."

She placed him in my arms as I wept for joy to hold him for the first time.

Those words rang over and over in my head. "Your baby has only a few hours to live." I was heartbroken. But my grieving would have to wait. Time was of the essence and I didn't want to miss one second with my sweet baby boy. We had only a few hours to make a lifetime of memories.

The hospital kindly gave us a large room for all of our family to gather in. While we eagerly waited for the nurse to bring our little son to us, we all prayed and cried together. As I sat there, I looked into each of our children's sad, tearful eyes and prayed that God would guard their hearts as they said good-bye to their little brother.

Soon the door opened and in walked the nurse holding a blue blanket wrapped around our precious Matthew. She placed him in my arms as I wept for joy to hold him for the first time. He was beautiful and looked so normal. How could this adorable little guy actually be dying? But, as they explained, his issues were all internal, not on the outside, which tricked my mind into thinking he wasn't really going to die. However, my heart knew he'd be gone soon and I needed to cement every precious moment of these few hours into my mind.

Lifetime of Memories

We began to pass him around so everyone would have a chance to love on him, study his little face, kiss on him, and tell him their final good-byes. The hours passed too quickly, and finally, when he was back in my husband's arms, he took his last breath. He was gone. Now at peace in heaven, our little Matthew was in the arms of Jesus. We all gave him one last kiss good-bye and then the nurse softly walked off with him.

Instead of bringing our sweet little Matthew home from the hospital to fill a lifetime of memories with us, we were sitting at his memorial service. The church was filled with many of our precious family and friends, who brought us great comfort and encouragement. It was a beautiful celebration of life as God's magnificent presence was felt by all.

But soon we were back home and the long road of emotional healing was before us. We all desperately clung to God and His Word as He graciously sustained us. "If your law had not been my delight, I would have perished in my affliction" (Psalm 119:92).

Acknowledge the Lies

Going through a trial like that can be emotionally exhausting, and many times we may experience spiritual weakness and can be vulnerable to the enemy's attacks. These hard situations might lead us to doubt God, to question His love, to become angry, to let bitterness well up in our hearts, to allow fear to take hold, and, for some, to even turn our backs on God, forgetting His faithfulness, and walk away.

> Suffering can leave an open door for doubt to the walk through. When suffering knocks on someone's door, Satan too comes knocking. Life is a war zone, and Satan is the enemy strategist. He waits for those times when people are in the wilderness— vulnerable, desperate, and God seemingly far away or absent altogether. That's when Satan's questions about God's character, which might seem silly during the good times, suddenly make

sense. Why would anyone entertain Satan's questions about God's goodness when everything is good? But a few bumps in the road, and our knowledge of God seems fragile, and that's what Satan is counting on.[23]

Put- Off / Put-On

But, years ago, I learned to use a very practical tool that helps me focus on His truth when I feel emotionally weak and vulnerable. I generally use this principle every day. It is the principle of "Put Off /Put On."

Let me show you how I use it in my life. First, I immediately acknowledge the lie and second, I quickly replace it with God's truth. For example, if I let my guard down during the emotionally hard days after Matthew's home-going, I could have easily allowed my mind to wander out of control and begun to question God's authority:

"Does God care? He let Matthew die."
"I am afraid of what tomorrow will bring."
"I feel hopeless."

Can you see the lies? But as I intentionally put off the lies and put on God's truth, I can stand strong against the lies. It's something that must be practiced habitually every day.

Here's an example of a "Put Off /Put On." I'll use the lies I mentioned earlier. "Does God care? He let Matthew die." "I am afraid what tomorrow will bring." "I feel hopeless."

Put Off - "God is not truly good or he would have healed Matthew."
Put On - "God is Good": "O give thanks to the LORD, for He is good; For His lovingkindness is everlasting" (1 Chronicles 16:34).

Put Off - "I am afraid."
Put On - "Don't Fear": "When I am afraid, I put my trust in You" (Psalm 56:3).

Put Off - "I feel so hopeless."
Put On - "My hope is in God. Surely there is a future, and your hope will not be cut off" (Proverbs 23:18 ESV).

Can you see the process? This simple principle helps me to check my heart regularly. Daily I ask God to let me see and combat the lies that so easily distract me and bring doubt. When we doubt God, we are questioning His character, the very essence of His authority, holiness, faithfulness, mercy, and grace. When I read Scripture, I always look for the "Put Off / Put On" principle. Look at the verse below. Let's see if you can pick out the "Put Off / Put On" principle God has for us.

"To put off your old self, which belongs to your former manner of life and is corrupt through deceitful desires, and to be renewed in the spirit of your minds, and to put on the new self, created after the likeness of God in true righteousness and holiness" (Ephesians 4:22–24 ESV).

Put Off:
Your old self
Your former way of life
Deceitful desires

Put On:
Be renewed in the Spirit and the Truth of God's Word.
The new self, created after the likeness of God in true righteousness and holiness

Truth Fights the Struggle

Once you get the hang of this, you will be amazed to see how God gives you so many principles in Scripture to help you put off the lie and put on the truth. Practice this when you read your Bible. Use the truth to help fight the struggle with temptations, doubt, and lies.

The battle with sin always starts in our minds. Our thoughts must be brought into submission because emotions begin with thoughts. We must choose the truth. It is a war that our adversary wants to win.

If we are serious about living a life that honors God, then we must consider what we are feeding our minds. Take time to review what you are allowing your mind to absorb each day. This next verse is a great filter through which to run your media, books, and music.

The battle with sin always starts in our minds.

"Finally, brothers, whatever is true, whatever is honorable, whatever is just, whatever is pure, whatever is lovely, whatever is commendable, if there is any excellence, if there is anything worthy of praise, think about these things" (Philippians 4:8). Print this verse and put it on your TV, on your computer, on the fridge, on your mirror, in the car, at the office and make it your screen saver.

We are in a spiritual battle. Use the ammunition of God's Word to combat the lies of the enemy. He is relentless, sneaky, and deceitful and wants to destroy you. Fill your mind with God's truth and push out the lies. God, in His goodness, chooses to sanctify us to be more like His Son.

> Sanctification is the call for us to put off the old self, one wrought with sin, and put on the new self, one filled by the Spirit. It is the process of our hearts, minds, and desires being brought into greater conformity with God's. Sanctification is the Christian's growth in grace. Sanctification means to become more Christlike, an aspiration that seems all but impossible to reach —but the Lord calls all Christians to holiness and Christlikeness.[24]

Choose to fight the battle by putting on God's truth, memorizing and meditating on Scripture, so when the unexpected hard times come, like our experience with Matthew, you can stand strong on the Word of God and His truth.

Put off lies and put on truth. Repeat!

Reflection:

◆ Stop and pray right now and ask God to graciously and kindly reveal the lies of your heart, the lies that you are believing over His truth.

◆ Write a list of the sins you need to put off and what truth you need to put on. Ask the Holy Spirit to bring to mind every lie that you have chosen to replace with God's truth, including lies about His character, His Word, and His Faithfulness. List the lies.

◆ One by one, acknowledge the lies you have been believing. Confess these to God. Then ask for His gracious forgiveness for each lie. Humbly ask God to forgive you for choosing to not believe Him. I John 1: 9 tells us that He promises to forgive us immediately when we ask.

◆ You can be free from these lies right now through the power of God in Christ Jesus. Freedom in Christ is graciously offered to you this very moment. State the truth that you must put on.

◆ Write out a prayer right now and then pray it back to God.

Day 2 - Put Off / Put On

* Make sure to have your Bible, Companion Journal, and pen.
* Pray before you start. Use the guided prayer.
* Open your Bible and read the Scripture selected for today.
* Begin learning your Scripture memory verse and review it throughout the week.

Prayer: Use this prayer as a guide.

> *Abba Father, thank You for allowing me to come into Your presence. I give thanks and praise to Your truth, Your Word, Your power. I stand alone on the truth of Your Living Word that combats the lies that I see I can easily believe. I love You. In the name of my Savior, Jesus, Amen.*

Recite your Scripture Memory - Psalm 119:127 – 128.

"Therefore I love your commandments above gold, above fine gold. Therefore I consider all your precepts to be right; I hate every false way."

Open your Bible to Psalm 119:1 – 48. Read the entire section one time through.

Look for "Put Off / Put On" truths in each passage you read.

Day 2 Questions - Use your Companion Journal to answer the questions.

1. According to Psalm 119: 1-6, what does David consider a man must do to be blessed? What must our eyes be fixed on?

2. In Psalm 119: 7-16, how much value does David give to God's words? List the ways you know this to be true.

3. How do you see David safeguarding his mind from evil in Psalm 119: 1-48?

4. Which of David's declarations in Psalm 119: 44-48 ring true in your own life? Why?

Meditate on Psalm 119:14 – 16.

"In the way of your testimonies I delight as much as in all riches. I will meditate on your precepts and fix my eyes on your ways. I will delight in your statutes; I will not forget your word."

Close this time in grateful worship and prayer.

Day 3 - Put on the Word of God

* Make sure to have your Bible, Companion Journal, and pen.

* Pray before you start. Use the guided prayer.

* Open your Bible and read the Scripture selected for today.

* Begin learning your Scripture memory verse and review it throughout the week.

Prayer: Use this prayer as a guide.

> *Lord God, I delight in Your word, my soul longs for Your truth. I praise You because You are the almighty God, who takes pleasure in Your children. Open my eyes to see wondrous things in Your Word today. I love You. In Jesus's name, Amen.*

Recite your Scripture Memory - Psalm 119:127 – 128.

"Therefore I love your commandments above gold, above fine gold. Therefore I consider all your precepts to be right; I hate every false way."

Open your Bible to Psalm 119:1 – 48. Read the entire section one time through.

Look for "Put Off / Put On" truths in each passage you read.

Day 3 Questions - Use your Companion Journal to answer the questions.

1. What are the words David uses to describe God's Word in Psalm 119: 41-48?

2. List all the ways David finds comfort in his affliction (see Psalm 119: 49-56).

3. Why does David feel his affliction was good for him (see Psalm 119: 65-72)?

4. How can we be an example to others and lead them to follow the truth (see Psalm 119: 73-80)?

5. Insert your name in every place you see the word "I" in Psalm 119: 49-80. Which of these would you most like to be true in your life and why?

Meditate on Psalm 119:34 – 36.

"Give me understanding, that I may keep your law and observe it with my whole heart. Lead me in the path of your commandments, for I delight in it. Incline my heart to your testimonies, and not to selfish gain!"

Close this time in grateful worship and prayer.

Day 4 - Put on the Word of God

* Make sure to have your Bible, Companion Journal, and pen.
* Pray before you start. Use the guided prayer.
* Open your Bible and read the Scripture selected for today.
* Begin learning your Scripture memory verse and review it throughout the week.

Prayer: Use this prayer as a guide.

> *God of all praise, I long for Your truth. Give me the insight to see the wisdom in Your Word. I desire to meditate on Your words so I might not sin against You. I trust in Your Word to lead me away from sinful thoughts. I treasure Your word in my heart. I am grateful for You. In the sinless name of Jesus, Amen.*

Recite your Scripture Memory - Psalm 119:127 – 128.

"Therefore I love your commandments above gold, above fine gold. Therefore I consider all your precepts to be right; I hate every false way."

Open your Bible to Psalm 119:1 – 48. Read the entire section one time through.

Look for "Put Off / Put On" truths in each passage you read.

Day 4 Questions - Use your Companion Journal to answer the questions.

1. What does David long for in Psalm 119: 81-88?

2. How does the enemy want to destroy you and what must you do to combat the lies (see Psalm 119: 88-104)?

3. Describe David's oath and commitment to keeping God's Word (see Psalm 119: 105-112).

4. How does David contrast evil and God's Word (see Psalm 119: 113-120)?

5. What does David see as the only weapon to combat the enemy (see Psalm 119: 121-128)?

Meditate on Psalm 119:127 - 128.

"Therefore I love your commandments above gold, above fine gold. Therefore I consider all your precepts to be right, I hate every false way."

Close this time in grateful worship and prayer.

Day 5 - Put on the Word of God.

* Make sure to have your Bible, Companion Journal, and pen.
* Pray before you start. Use the guided prayer.
* Open your Bible and read the Scripture selected for today.
* Begin learning your Scripture memory verse and review it throughout the week.

Prayer: Use this prayer as a guide.

> *Dear faithful Father, Your Word is steadfast, comforting, encouraging, and protective. You love me enough to guide me through Your wisdom so I stay on the right path. Oh God, in Your mercy, lead me through Your Word and let me see Your promises. You are good. In Jesus's powerful name, Amen.*

Recite your Scripture Memory - Psalm 119:127 – 128.

"Therefore I love your commandments above gold, above fine gold. Therefore I consider all your precepts to be right; I hate every false way."

Open your Bible to Psalm 119:1 – 48. Read the entire section one time through.

Look for "Put Off / Put On" truths in each passage you read.

Day 5 Questions - Use your Companion Journal to answer the questions.

1. Describe some of David's own words of passion for God's Word (see Psalm 119: 129–144).

2. List contrasts or similarities between your love for God's Word and David's love for God's Word (see Psalm 119: 145–160).

3. In verses 161–168, what does David purpose to do to stay close to God and His Word?

4. Describe David's humility in Psalm 119: 169–176.

5. What is the overriding theme in Psalm 119: 119? What does David choose to put off in his life and what does he put on?

Meditate on Psalm 119:131 – 133.

"I open my mouth and pant, because I long for your commandments. Turn to me and be gracious to me, as is your way with those who love your name. Keep steady my steps according to your promises and let no iniquity get dominion over me."

Close this time in grateful worship and prayer.

Day 6 - The Good Portion - A Time of Worship

This is the day of the week that you do as Mary did and sit for an extended amount of time in prayer and worship. Block out at least an hour, perhaps more, once a week, to have extended time to be still, sit quietly all by yourself, and simply worship your Father.

Use Psalm 119 to guide your praise for God.

1. Praise (Use Psalm 119 to guide you).

2. Gratitude (Use Psalm 119 to guide you).

3. Worship (Sing).

4. Cry out to God with the lies you are believing and ask His forgiveness (ACTS - Adoration, Confession, Thanksgiving, and Supplication).

5. Recite one of your Scriptures back to God from memory. Hiding God's Word in your heart is a beautiful way to show God that you value Him and His thoughts.

6. Write out a closing prayer committing to believing God's truth alone.

9
Habitual Sins

9 Habitual Sins

Chapter 9 - Bondage

Day 1

* Make sure to have your Bible, Companion Journal, and pen.
* Pray before you start.
* Open your Bible and read the Scripture selected for today.
* Read Chapter 9 of <u>The Good Portion</u>.
* Begin learning your Scripture memory verse so you will be ready to recite it on Day 6.

Scripture Reading - Luke 7:36 – 50

Scripture Memory - Psalm 25:4, 5.

"Make me to know your ways, O Lord teach me your paths. Lead me in your truth and teach me, for you are the God of my salvation; for you I wait all the day long."

Chapter 9

Beautiful Shelly

Shelly was a beautiful, thin, redhead with gorgeous green eyes. Everywhere she went, people took notice. She could hardly walk into a room without everyone stopping to look. She hated the stares, but secretly it fed her desire to be accepted. In junior high school, all the boys took notice of her and she took notice of them.

Shelly's parents had divorced when she was just five years old, and both parents were quite busy and too distracted with their jobs to give much time or attention to her and her siblings. She felt as though she was on her own to do whatever she wanted.

With not much guidance, Shelly began to do what was right in her own eyes. Her beauty gained her plenty of attention from the young men. She was introduced to drugs by some friends she met at a party. Sadly, her life of sex, drugs, and a longing for love continued right into college.

While in her sophomore year, she met Allen. He seemed so different from the other guys. He was polite, gentlemanly, and protective. She was smitten from the get-go. He was truly the prince she had longed for.

Soon, Shelly was in her elegant wedding dress, walking down the aisle on the arm of her dad, headed toward her prince, who looked regal in his black tuxedo. Allen was staring intently at her with a hint of a smile on his face. She was all smiles and had tears of joy in her eyes. This was the best day of her life.

Off to the Caribbean they went for a two-week honeymoon. Shelly felt like she was in heaven. The white powdered sand beneath her feet and the crystal-clear emerald water splashing around her ankles as the sun was setting on the horizon was truly too picturesque for words.

Shelly's Nightmare Honeymoon

On day three of their fairy-tale honeymoon, the beautiful married life Shelly had dreamed of came to a crashing halt. She and Allen were standing in line for a reservation at a swanky restaurant when the young maitre d' made a few comments about Shelly's beauty. Allen did not appreciate this man's flirtatious behavior and grabbed Shelly's arm extremely tight and told her to stop making eye contact with the maitre d'. For a moment, Shelly felt hurt by his accusations, but then she realized that he was just being protective in a jealous kind of way. She thought it was rather cute.

After dinner, the maitre d' made another comment that did not sit well with Allen, but he seemed to just brush it off until they were back in their hotel room. At that point Allen became very angry with Shelly and pushed her up against the wall, accusing her of being unfaithful to him. He then began to hit her and threaten her. He said she was worthless without him and that he had only married her out of pity. It was a nightmare. She couldn't believe this was the same man. Was she dreaming? How could this be happening to her?

The abuse continued for years, and Allen threatened her to tell no one. Frightened, Shelly turned to drugs and alcohol again, to ease the pain, hurt, and rejection. One day, she could not take it anymore. The drugs and alcohol were ruining her health, so she turned to God for help. She felt utterly trapped and imprisoned. She cried for days at the hopelessness of her horrible situation.

> .She couldn't believe this was the same man. Was she dreaming?

She soon visited a church around the corner and unleashed the ugly truth about her drug and alcohol addiction to the pastor. Because of gripping fear, she never told anyone about the physical and emotional abuse that occurred. After all, Allen had stopped the physical abuse a few years before, but, now he had settled into being indifferent, disconnected and emotionally abusive. Shelly felt like damaged goods, worthless and afraid. She had a lot of guilt and shame over the many sinful decisions she had made. Shelly continued to struggle with many habitual sins. Her drinking and drug usage continued. She felt trapped in a life that wasn't worth living most days.

Shelly's Secrets and Cry for Help

One day, I received a call from a good friend who was concerned about Shelly, whom she had just met at church the previous Sunday. She wanted to know if I would meet with Shelly. I made room on my calendar, and the following Friday, she was sitting across from me.

Shelly took me on a journey through her life and told me about her past, including the drugs, alcohol, and fornication. She never even hinted at the emotional abuse going on at home. On the contrary, she spoke very highly of Allen and their marriage. But, because I've counseled women for years, it's pretty easy to pick up on the signs and hints of deeper issues.

I knew we needed to work through a lot, and Shelly seemed open and willing to get started right away. She had come to her end, sick of her life. The habitual sins that had long made her feel hopeless, shameful, and guilty were driving her to the loving feet of Jesus. She wanted His healing, forgiveness, and freedom desperately in her life.

They Gave Her a Rough Title

Let's read about another woman who was in a similar situation to Shelly. This woman had also been trapped in the bondage of sin for many years, most of her life to be exact. She was known as "a woman who was a sinner." That's a pretty rough title. Her story is remarkable.

Let's meet this "woman who was a sinner" in the pages of Luke. Open your Bible to Luke 7:36–50 and read these verses before you continue. We pick up the story in Galilee. Jesus was ministering in the area and was invited to dine at Simon the Pharisee's home. This man, Simon, being curious, wanted to host Him for dinner. Jesus accepted the invitation, even though others thought it was inappropriate for Him to dine with publicans and sinners.

"One of the Pharisees asked him [Jesus] to eat with him, and he went into the Pharisee's house and reclined at the table" (Luke 7:36).

Now, here's where the woman, known as "a sinner," enters into our story. This mysterious woman was known in the city as a prostitute. Her reputation had defined her as unworthy, unclean, and rejected for many years. She was use to the degrading remarks from others, with the sneers, the laughs, and all the mocking.

She was going to see Jesus and nothing was going to stop her.

Now this woman was on a mission to find Jesus. She had heard that He was unconditionally loving, merciful, and forgiving. She desperately wanted to find Him. She knew Jesus was the only one who could forgive her sins and free her from the bondage to a life of shame, guilt, and rejection. She must find Him.

One day as she strolled down the back streets of her city, she heard that Jesus was nearby. She asked around urgently in hopes of finding out where he might be. Soon she got wind that He was at Simon's home.

At that moment, she knew she must see Him. She must. Nothing would stop her from seeing Him. Most would have thought it a really bad idea to go to Simon's house. Some might have even reminded her that she was a harlot and that it was culturally inappropriate for her to enter Simon's house uninvited. It was a very risky idea, for sure. But she never counted the cost or risk. She was going to see Jesus and nothing was going to stop her.

As the men were conversing and enjoying a nice meal, the door opened and this woman, "the sinner, the harlot, the prostitute, the unworthy woman," quietly and humbly walked right into the room with absolutely no hesitation. "And behold, a woman of the city, who was a sinner, when she learned that he was reclining at the table in the Pharisee's house, came in" (Luke 7:37a).

Tresses of Beauty

This next scene brings tears to my eyes every time I read it: "and standing behind him at his feet, weeping, she began to wet his feet with her tears and wiped them with the hair of her head and kissed his feet and anointed them with the ointment" (verse 37).

 She walks in and weeps at the sight of Jesus. This woman knew her sins were great, but she also knew Who was greater and could set her free. She saw Jesus as her Hope and Redeemer. She entered the room crying and with a contrite, humble heart and desired nothing more than to fall before Jesus and fervently kiss His feet. Noticing that her tears had wet His feet, she let her hair down to wipe them. Her long hair, tresses of her beauty, which had snared many a man in her past, was now being used as a towel to wipe the tears that wet the Savior's feet.

I can't think of a more beautiful picture of true humility and pure worship before the Lord Jesus. This scene humbled me and challenged my view of personal worship before the Savior. Am I unashamed to fall on my face in worship of my sweet Savior? Do I know my sin is great before a holy God and do I see my need to run to Him in need of His forgiveness and grace?

This woman, in Luke 7, knew the only hope of breaking free from the bondage of her sin and the life in which she felt trapped was to come to Jesus. She knew He was the only hope for true joy, contentment, and a changed heart. For the first time, she saw the wretchedness of her own sinful heart compared to the righteousness of Jesus. She stopped seeing herself through others' opinions of her. How they defined her didn't matter anymore. She wanted to see herself in the light of who Jesus was. She knew this Man wanted to free her and had the power to do so. She just wanted to live in victory over her sin and be free to worship Him. She wanted to be valued by her Savior.

But, unfortunately, the Pharisees still had a problem with this woman. Her reputation as a harlot clung to her, and she was a very unwelcome intruder in Simon's house. Verses 39–40 tell us, "Now when the Pharisee who had invited him saw this, he said to himself, If this man were a prophet, he would have known who and what sort of woman this is who is touching him, for she is a sinner."

Defined by Her Past

These men did not approve of this wretched woman coming in and disrupting their dinner. These men had defined her as worthless and labeled her as a "sinner." They saw themselves as better than she. But look at Jesus's response as He turned toward the woman and asked Simon to look at her.

> Do you see this woman? I entered your house; you gave me no water for my feet, but she has wet my feet with her tears and wiped them with her hair. You gave me no kiss, but from the time I came in she has not ceased to kiss my feet. You did not anoint my head with oil, but she has anointed my feet with ointment. Therefore I tell you, her sins, which are many, are forgiven—for she loved much. But he who is forgiven little, loves little." And he said to her, "Your sins are forgiven." Then those who were at table with him began to say among themselves, "Who is this, who even forgives sins?" And he said to the woman, "Your faith has saved you; go in peace" (Luke 43–50).

Wow. What an incredibly beautiful picture of Jesus's compassion and unconditional love. He didn't condemn her, criticize her, or rehash her past, He simply encouraged everyone present to take notice of her humble, contrite, repentant heart. He was illuminating the contrast between their prideful, arrogant hearts and her surrendered heart. Jesus then turned to her and gently said with all the power of heaven, "Your faith has saved you; go in peace" (Luke 43–50).

The glorious transformation of her new identity now declared her as forgiven...

Can you just imagine how immense her joy must have been as she left the house that day? She came to Jesus as a prostitute, labeled a "sinner," devalued, unloved, shamed, used, abused, and rejected. The glorious transformation of her new identity now declared her as forgiven, redeemed, valued, loved, and set free through the powerful grace of Jesus! She was free to live as a child of God because Jesus declared her His.

She had been labeled *a woman who was a sinner* and now she was to be labeled *a child of the Most High God*, through Jesus Christ, her Lord and Savior.

Maybe you feel like this woman, or maybe you feel like our friend Shelly. Ask yourself this: does your sin make you want to fall on your face before a holy God or run away from Him? Most people feel the guilt of their sin in the presence of a holy God and they run out fear of judgment.

We have been set free to reflect Christ, but when we choose to live in sin, we place ourselves in bondage and control to that sin. We reflect the characteristics of that sin. When we see our sin as wicked in light of a holy God and truly want to be free, we run to Him in humility, not away.

This is what it looks like:

Habitual Sinner - Has guilt of Sin - Looks to Holy God - Runs from Holy God - Continues in Habitual Sins - Has More Guilt

Habitual Sinner - Has guilt of Sin - Looks to Holy God - Runs toward Holy God - Repents - Confesses - Receives Forgiveness - Lives in Freedom

Habitually sinning in an area, such as, pornography, bitterness, eating too much or too little, purposely harming our bodies, spending too much money, spending too much time on media devices, obsessing about our outward appearance, drunkenness, ungodly use of sex, gossip, cursing, outbursts of anger, and so on, is defined as a behavioral issue that points to a sinful, idolatrous heart. We rely on and worship these idols to fulfill the lust of our flesh. Sadly, we choose to worship these idols in place of worshipping God. We allow our habitual sins to hinder our relationship with God.

> When we examine our hearts, we find that the greatest danger is that we are hooked on ourselves. If I am an alcoholic, my ultimate idol is not the bottle. It is I. I idolize myself. My desires are of first importance. My cravings rule – cravings for popularity, freedom from pain, revenge, or freedom from frustrations at home or work. Addiction is self-worship. This means that even if I give up alcohol, unless I deal head on with my biggest problem, I will never truly find freedom. I will just find something else to serve my desires.[25]

"Behold, the Lord's hand is not shortened, that it cannot save, or his ear dull, that it cannot hear; but your iniquities have made a separation between you and your God, and your sins have hidden his face from you so that he does not hear. For your hands are defiled with blood and your fingers with iniquity; your lips have spoken lies; your tongue mutters wickedness" (Isaiah 59:1–3).

As believers we are not under the judgment or wrath of God, and we have been labeled *righteous* because of Jesus. Unfortunately, we will be continually tempted in our flesh to sin, but God, in His mercy and grace, chooses to sanctify us daily through the power of Jesus's name.

Have you ever tried to stop overeating, stop looking at pornography, or stop drinking, smoking, lying, or gossiping on your own? It's tough. When you have been habitually feeding your flesh to satisfy your emotions, the habitual sin gains a stronghold on you that puts you in bondage to it. That is a stronghold that only God can free you from. You must have the power of God to be freed from the idols of your heart.

> Using the perspective of idolatry, addicts are blinded by their own desire. They refuse to see themselves as dependent on God. God's glory and fame is not their goal. In their self-addiction or selfishness, they worship and bow down before false gods. Addicts have defected from the living God. Instead of worshipping in the temple of the Lord, they perform addictive rituals that give them more perceived power, pleasure, or identity. They see in their addiction a form of magic (Deut. 18:10-14). The promises of the idol, however, are lies. Any identity, power, or peace they bring is false and temporary. There are only two choices: putting your faith in a loving God and thus knowing freedom, or putting your faith in idols (Satan) and being enslaved. Curiously, our selfish pride prefers slavery. [26]

In Hebrews 4:16, Paul encourages us, "Let us then with confidence draw near to the throne of grace, that we may receive mercy and find grace to help in time of need."

Shelly and I continued to meet each week, and she began to see through the powerful pages of Scripture just how much her Savior loved and valued her and how her unconfessed sin was hindering her ability to see God's truth.

Shelly needed to put to death her sinful patterns and replace them with life-giving, God-honoring habits. She had to take the time to deal with these habitual sins head-on.

You must have the power of God to be freed from the idols of your hearts.

I suggested Shelly choose a day, find a quiet place, and take a personal sabbatical. This is a time to go before God and fall before Him in utter surrender and allow Him to free her.

Shelly did just that. She decided to take a personal sabbatical. She took a day off from work, collected her Bible, a notebook, a pen, and her water bottle, found a quiet room in her house, closed the door, got on her knees, and fell humbly before the mercy and grace of Jesus. She immediately started sobbing, as her heart was so humbled to finally be alone with God.

Shelly Sat There Weeping on Her Knees

Shelly saw herself for the first time, so helpless, so heartbroken, so shamed, so trapped in bondage to her sin. God graciously allowed her heart to be broken over her sin, the lies she believed, the degrading, shameful label she allowed others to stick on her. Her eyes were opened to the guilt of so many wrong choices she had made, the bitterness that had taken root in her heart, and the shame she felt over her prideful heart that had rejected His truth.

Shelly fell at Jesus's feet that day and surrendered it all to Him. One by one, in the name of Jesus, she confessed, repented, and asked God, in His great mercy, to forgive her for each sin she had committed against her holy Father. In Hebrews 4:16, Paul encourages us, "Let us then with confidence draw near to the throne of grace, that we may receive mercy and find grace to help in time of need."

Shelly sat there weeping on her knees, with her face in her hands, crying out for His forgiveness. She knew He did forgive her, but it would take time for her to walk through all of the areas of her heart.

> A sincere heart and a desire to know the Lord more deeply and richly is all that is needed for the Lord to work through our stubbornness and seeking after that which we know will not ultimately satisfy us. It is not our will or determination that evokes transformation and growth but the loving-kindness of the Lord. Even when our sanctification seems slow, the Lord is faithful to initiate and bring change.[27]

We are not meant to do this life alone. We need one another to continue on this progressive sanctifying road we are all on. We need to seek wise counsel and accountability from more mature believers who can guide us to complete freedom from the areas that we all struggle with. We all go through seasons of spiritual weakness and we just need help. I highly recommend looking into the Association of Certified Biblical Counselors in your area for help (see biblicalcounseling.com).

My Prayer for You

> "That the God of our Lord Jesus Christ, the Father of glory, may give you the Spirit of wisdom and of revelation in the knowledge of him, having the eyes of your hearts enlightened, that you may know what is the hope to which he has called you, what are the

riches of his glorious inheritance in the saints, and what is the immeasurable greatness of his power toward us who believe, according to the working of his great might that he worked in Christ when he raised him from the dead" (Ephesians1:16–20).

Reflection:

◆ Stop and pray right now and ask God to graciously and kindly reveal the habitual sins that you feel powerless to overcome. Habitual sins are cycles of sin we repeat over and over. We either feel we can't overcome them or we never even bother to try.

◆ Write a list of the habitual sins that you struggle with.

◆ One by one, acknowledge the lies you have been believing. Confess these to God. Then ask for His gracious forgiveness for each lie. Humbly ask God to forgive you for choosing to not believe God. I John 1: 9 tells us that He promises to forgive us immediately when we ask.

◆ You can be free from these lies right now through the power of God in Christ Jesus. Freedom in Christ is graciously offered to you this very moment.

◆ Write out a prayer right now and then pray it back to God.

Day 2 - Desire God

* Make sure to have your Bible, Companion Journal, and pen.
* Pray before you start. Use the guided prayer.
* Open your Bible and read the Scripture selected for today.
* Begin learning your Scripture memory verse and review it throughout the week.

Prayer: Use this prayer as a guide. The prayers in this section will be the prayers of David out of the Psalms.

> *"Hear me, Lord, and answer me, for I am poor and needy. Guard my life, for I am faithful to you; save your servant who trusts in you. You are my God; have mercy on me, Lord, for I call to you all day long. Bring joy to your servant, Lord, for I put my trust in you." (Psalm 86:1–4)*

Recite your Scripture Memory - Psalm 25:4, 5.

"Make me to know your ways, O Lord teach me your paths. Lead me in your truth and teach me, for you are the God of my salvation; for you I wait all the day long."

Open your Bible to Psalm 25. Read the entire chapter one time through.

Day 2 Questions - Use your notebook to answer the questions.

1. Describe, in your own words, David's relationship with God.

2. In Psalm 25; 1 - 2, what words are used to show David's surrender to God?

3. What are the promises in Psalm 119: 3? Why is that important to you?

4. Why is shame such a big deal to David?

5. Describe a time you felt great shame.

Meditate on Psalm 25:1 – 4.

"To you, O Lord, I lift up my soul. O my God, in you I trust; let me not be put to shame; let not my enemies exult over me. Indeed, none who wait for you shall be put to shame; they shall be ashamed who are wantonly treacherous."

Close this time in grateful worship and prayer.

Day 3 - Desire God

✱ Make sure to have your Bible, Companion Journal, and pen.

✱ Pray before you start. Use the guided prayer.

✱ Open your Bible and read the Scripture selected for today.

✱ Begin learning your Scripture memory verse and review it throughout the week.

Prayer: Use this prayer as a guide.

> *"You, Lord, are forgiving and good, abounding in love to all who call to you. Hear my prayer, Lord listen to my cry for mercy. When I am distress, I call to you, because you answer me"(Psalm 86:5–7).*

Recite your Scripture Memory - Psalm 25:4, 5.

"Make me to know your ways, O Lord teach me your paths. Lead me in your truth and teach me, for you are the God of my salvation; for you I wait all the day long."

Open your Bible to Psalm 25. Read the entire chapter one time through.

Day 3 Questions - Use your Companion Journal to answer the questions.

1. David is a learned man, but even he asks to be taught by God. What are the three things David wants from God?

2. Rewrite those verses putting your name in the place of "me"
(Make _____ to know your ways ...). Stop and pray. Ask God to make this true in your own heart (see Psalm 25: 4, 5).

3. In Psalm 25: 6 and 7, write down the three things David wants God to remember.

4. How does David describe God's character in Psalm 25: 8-10? What does God do? List all of the actions you see God take in these verses.

5. Describe God's steadfast love. How do you see His steadfast love in your life?

Meditate on Psalm 25:8 – 10.

"Good and upright is the Lord; therefore he instructs sinners in the way. He leads the humble in what is right, and teaches the humble his way. All the paths of the Lord are steadfast love and faithfulness, for those who keep his covenant and his testimonies."

Close this time in grateful worship and prayer.

Day 4 - Desire God

* Make sure to have your Bible, Companion Journal, and pen.
* Pray before you start. Use the guided prayer.
* Open your Bible and read the Scripture reading for today.
* Begin learning your Scripture memory verse and review it throughout the week.

Prayer: Use this prayer as a guide.

> *"Teach me your way, Lord, that I may rely on your faithfulness, give me an undivided heart, that I may fear your name; I will praise you, Lord, my God, with all my heart; I will glorify your name forever" (Psalm 86:11, 12).*

Recite your Scripture Memory - Psalm 25:4, 5.

"Make me to know your ways, O Lord teach me your paths. Lead me in your truth and teach me, for you are the God of my salvation; for you I wait all the day long."

Open your Bible to Psalm 25. Read the entire chapter one time through.

Day 4 Questions - Use your Companion Journal to answer the questions.

1. What is the difference between doubt and trust and what ways to you struggle with doubt?

2. What happens when we doubt God's Word (see 2 Timothy 4:3-5)?

3. Eve's first mistake was to talk with Satan. We should never entertain anything that encourages us to doubt God. Every word of man should be examined through the filter of the Bible. God's Word is the final authority. How might you be encouraging your mind to be distracted by lies (maybe social media, movies, books)? List your weaknesses below.

4. Write out a commitment to God asking Him to give you strength and wisdom to be on your guard against the lies of the enemy.

Meditate on Psalm 25:12.

"Who is the man who fears the Lord? Him will he instruct in the way that he should choose."

Close this time in grateful worship and prayer.

Day 5 - Desire God

* Make sure to have your Bible, Companion Journal, and pen.
* Pray before you start. Use the guided prayer.
* Open your Bible and read the Scripture reading for today.
* Begin learning your Scripture memory verse and review it throughout the week.

Prayer: Use this prayer as a guide.

> *"But you, Lord, are a compassionate and gracious God, slow to anger, abounding in love and faithfulness. Turn to me and have mercy on me; show your strength on behalf of your servant." (Psalm 86:15, 16)*

Recite your Scripture Memory - Psalm 25:4, 5.

"Make me to know your ways, O Lord teach me your paths. Lead me in your truth and teach me, for you are the God of my salvation; for you I wait all the day long."

Open your Bible to Psalm 25. Read the entire chapter one time through.

Day 5 Questions - Use your Companion Journal to answer the questions.

1. List all the benefits for those who fear the Lord (see Psalm 25: 12-15).

2. David is clearly distressed in Psalm 25: 16-18. List all of David's issues and what he asks of the Lord for each issue.

3. Of all of David's issues, which did you relate to the most? Why (see Psalm 25: 16-19)?

4. Look through the chapter again and describe David's relationship with God? Why do you think David has that type of relationship with God?

5. After reading this Psalm, do you feel you could surrender your habitual sins to God? Why or why not?

Meditate on Psalm 25:4, 5.

"Make me to know your ways, O Lord; teach me your paths. Lead me in your truth and teach me, for you are the God of my salvation; for you I wait all the day long."

Close this time in grateful worship and prayer.

Day 6 - The Good Portion - A Time of Worship

This is the day of the week that you do as Mary did and sit for an extended amount of time in prayer and worship. Block out at least an hour, perhaps more, once a week, to have extended time to be still, sit quietly all by yourself, and simply worship your Father.

Use Psalm 25 to guide your praise for God.

1. Praise (Use Psalm 25 to guide you).

2. Gratitude (Use Psalm 25 to guide you).

3. Worship (Sing).

4. Cry out to God with the lies you are believing and ask His forgiveness
(ACTS - Adoration, Confession, Thanksgiving, and Supplication).

5. Recite one of your Scriptures back to God from memory. Hiding God's Word in your heart is a beautiful way to show God that you value Him and His thoughts.

6. Write out a closing prayer committing to believing God's truth alone.

10
Personal Sabbatical

10 Personal Sabbatical

Chapter 10 - Personal Sabbatical

Remember my friend Shelly, whom I mentioned in the previous chapter? Shelly set aside a day to take a personal sabbatical. Part of the process in my counseling women, and the point of this book, is to help believers like you to see God through new lenses, to define themselves biblically, to have their eyes open to the truth of God's Word, and to learn to hate sin and break free from habitual sins and idolatrous desires.

My sweet sister, you are a beautiful child of God, and you have been redeemed, justified, and stamped with the righteousness of Christ. You have been set apart for holiness! Let me repeat this statement:

> A sincere heart and a desire to know the Lord more deeply and richly is all that is needed for the Lord to work through our stubbornness and seeking after that which we know will not ultimately satisfy us. It is not our will or determination that evokes transformation and growth but the loving-kindness of the Lord. Even when our sanctification seems slow, the Lord is faithful to initiate and bring change. [28]

1 Thessalonians 5:23–24 tells us, "Now may the God of peace himself sanctify you completely, and may your whole spirit and soul and body be kept blameless at the coming of our Lord Jesus Christ. He who calls you is faithful; he will surely do it."

Ultimately, I desire to see women passionately worshipping God above all else. But, sadly, many are trapped in habitual sins and are choosing to worship the idols of their hearts.

Habitual sins are spiritual issues of our heart that dominate, enslave, and can destroy us. We just can't seem to overcome them, no matter how hard we try. We muster up control for a while, but we find ourselves back in the sin again and again.

Taking a Personal Sabbatical gives you much needed time to be quiet and still before your heavenly Father and allow Him to reveal the ugliness of your sinful desires. If you truly want to be freed from the bondage of these habitual sins, you must be intentional.

Habitual sins will reveal the idols you choose to worship. Look at this list and see if you might be struggling with any of these.

Food obsession (eating too much or too little)
drugs/alcohol
busyness
appearance
gossip
social media
sex
pornography
technology
anger
revenge
envy
fear

Does the thought of any of these stir a guilty response in your heart?

God wants to set you free from the habitual sins you are holding on to and afraid of letting go of. The fear of letting go and failing again is too discouraging. You are correct. The problem is your lack of understanding of God's character, the truth of His Word, and the power you have in Christ to overcome ALL sin.

Not dealing with the habitual sin, is like putting a tiny little Band-aid on a 5 inch gash on your leg. Soon infection sets in and then you have a huge problem, that requires emergency attention.

Your desire to be set free must come from a heart that desperately wants to worship and adore God and Him ONLY. Like Paul, you must passionately hate sin and desire God.

"Let not sin therefore reign in your mortal body, to make you obey its passions. Do not present your members to sin as instruments for unrighteousness, but present yourselves to God as those who have been brought from death to life, and your

members to God as instruments for righteousness. For sin will have no dominion over you, since you are not under law but under grace" (Romans 6:12-14).

"But thanks be to God, that you who were once slaves of sin have become obedient from the heart to the standard of teaching to which you were committed, and, having been set free from sin, have become slaves of righteousness" (Romans 6:17,18).

Personal Sabbatical

Guide to Breaking the Stronghold of Sin

Like my friend Shelly, I would suggest you take a personal sabbatical and deal with your bondage to sin.

Suggested Preparations for Your Personal Sabbatical:

✦ Choose a day to take your personal sabbatical and put it on the calendar.

✦ Choose a safe, quiet place to have your sabbatical, a place that you will not be interrupted.

✦ Collect your Bible, this book, The Good Portion, Companion Journal, a pen, a watch, (leave your phone and technology elsewhere), and plenty of water to drink.

✦ Fasting is usually a good idea during your sabbatical, but not if you have a health issue that would prevent you from doing so.

✦ You will use your notebook to do all your writing. This book is not designed to write in, so you may use it as a guide for future sabbaticals.

✦ Once in your sabbatical, following the step-by-step guide.

Guide to Breaking the Stronghold of Sin

1. Prayer

Start with a guided prayer. Satan cannot read your thoughts, so it is important that you speak your prayers to God audibly.

> *Dear Graciously Heavenly Father, I am humbled to come into Your presence and sit before You. Through the death, burial, and resurrection of Jesus Christ, I come before You. I ask You, in the name of Jesus and on His authority alone, that Satan, any evil spirits, demons, and any principalities of darkness be removed from my presence and have no influence over me. I ask You, almighty God, through Your Son Jesus Christ, to reign in this place. May my heart be open to Your Truth today and may all of the enemy's lies be removed. I commit this time to You. In the powerful name of Jesus Christ I pray, Amen.*

2. Scripture Reading

Open your Bible to Romans 6. Read this chapter aloud once, then pray, thanking God for His truth. Now, read the chapter again.

3. Notebook

Open your notebook. On the first page write the title, date, and time of this sabbatical.

4. Prayer of Gratitude

On the next page, Use Romans 6 as a guide to help you write out a prayer of gratitude for the freedom to be dead to sin and alive in Christ. Be specific in your prayer. Use as much time as you need.

5. Overview

Turn to the next empty page in your notebook and, using Romans 6, write down an overview of what it means to you to not be a slave to sin and to be alive in Christ. Pray again, and thank God for His Son Jesus, who redeemed you from eternity in hell and gave you the free gift of eternal life in heaven.

6. Attributes of God

Read each attribute of God along with the verse in your Bible. Praise and thank Him, one by one, for each one.

God is Holy - 1 Peter 1:15
God is Creator - Genesis 1:1
God is Love – 1 John 4:8
God never changes - Hebrews 13:8
God is Patient - 2 Peter 3:9
God is Light - 1 John 1:5
God is Perfect - Psalm 18:30
God is Truth - John 14:6
God is Spirit - John 4:24
God is Compassionate - Micah 7:18–19
God is our Strength - Isaiah 41:10
God is Faithful – 1 Corinthians 10:13
God is Peace - Philippians 4:7

7. My Position in Christ

When you trusted Jesus to be your Savior, God stamped you with the label "righteous." The blood of Jesus covers you with His righteousness. You are no longer condemned by your sin but rather made alive in Christ. But God, in His great mercy, saves us from the power of sin as well; this is called sanctification. Sanctification is not a one-time event. Sanctification is a lifelong journey. As a child of God, you are being sanctified to be more like Christ. Read the "My Position in Christ" chart below once through. Write in your notebook what you think about your position, how that makes you feel, and what you think God thinks about you.

• I am a child of God. "But to all who have received him--those who believe in his name--he has given the right to become God's children" (John 1:12).	**• I am redeemed and forgiven by the grace of Christ.** "In him we have redemption through his blood, the forgiveness of our trespasses, according to the riches of his grace" (Eph. 1:7).
• I am a branch of the true vine, and a conduit of Christ's life. "I am the true vine and my Father is the gardener. I am the vine; you are the branches. The one who remains in me--and I in him--bears much fruit, because apart from me you can accomplish nothing" (John 15:1, 5).	**• I have been sealed with the Holy Spirit of promise.** "And when you heard the word of truth (the gospel of your salvation)--when you believed in Christ--you were marked with the seal of the promised Holy Spirit" (Ephesians 1:13).
• I am a friend of Jesus. "I no longer call you slaves, because the slave does not understand what his master is doing. But I have called you friends, because I have revealed to you everything I heard from my Father" (John 15:15).	**• Because of God's mercy and love, I have been made alive with Christ.** "But God, being rich in mercy, because of his great love with which he loved us, even though we were dead in transgressions, made us alive together with Christ--by grace you are saved" (Ephesians 2:4-5).
• I have been justified and redeemed. "But they are justified freely by his grace through the redemption that is in Christ Jesus" (Romans 3:24).	**• I am a citizen of heaven.** "But our citizenship is in heaven--and we also await a savior from there, the Lord Jesus Christ" (Philippians 3:20).

• **My old self was crucified with Christ, and I am no longer a slave to sin.** "But they are justified freely by his grace through the redemption that is in Christ Jesus" (Romans 3:24).	• **The peace of God guards my heart and mind.** "And the peace of God that surpasses all understanding will guard your hearts and minds in Christ Jesus" (Philippians 4:7).
• **I will not be condemned by God.** "For the law of the life-giving Spirit in Christ Jesus has set you free from the law of sin and death" (Romans 8:2).	• **I have been made complete in Christ.** "You have been filled in him, who is the head over every ruler and authority" (Colossians 2:10).
• **As a child of God, I am a fellow heir with Christ.** "And if children, then heirs (namely, heirs of God and also fellow heirs with Christ)--if indeed we suffer with him so we may also be glorified with Him" (Romans 8:17).	• **God supplies all my needs.** "And my God will supply your every need according to his glorious riches in Christ Jesus" (Philippians 4:19).
• **I have been accepted by Christ.** "Receive one another, then, just as Christ also received you, to God's glory" (Romans 15:7). Copyright 2019 Heidi Baird. All rights reserved.	• **I am God's workmanship created to produce good works.** "For we are his workmanship, having been created in Christ Jesus for good works that God prepared beforehand that we should walk in them" (Ephesians 2:10).

8. Digging Deeper

This next part in your sabbatical is where you will dig deep into the sins of your heart. There are many steps, so follow the guided suggestions carefully.

Steps to follow:

Ask the Holy Spirit to search your heart and reveal the habitual sins you are holding onto before you start.

Use the two prayers at the end of section 8 as a guide.
A. Prayer to be used BEFORE each section:
B. Prayer to be used AFTER each section:

Begin to list the sins that come to mind under that particular heading:

Lies, Fear, Idols, Bitterness, Anger, Habitual Sins

If you hit a dead end and can't think of any more to add to the list, sit quietly for a few minutes and ask God to bring to mind anything you might be missing. Write down anything else you come up with. This might take a while, so do not rush through this section.

Write down the names of people whom you have offended and those who may have offended you and put a star by their names. Later, you will want to reach out to them and ask for their forgiveness if you have sinned against them.

Use the chapters in *The Good Portion* to help clarify any confusion you might have about any particular root issue. The chart on the next page will help guide you through the root issues.

Sin	Truth	Lies I Believe
Identity	Psalm 139:3,4	What is my worth? Who do I let define me? What do others say about me? What do I think about me?
Lies	Proverbs 30:5	What lies do I believe most often about myself? What lies to I most believe about God? Why do I believe lies? Who lies the most to me?
Fear	Psalm 111:10	What am I afraid of in my past? What am I afraid of in my future? Who am I afraid of? What scares me the most?
Idols	Isaiah 42:8	What am I afraid of losing? What do I think about the most? What can't I live without? Who's opinions do I care the most about?
Bitterness	Ephesians 4:31-32	Who am I withholding forgiveness from? Why? Who do I need to forgive don't want to? Why?
Anger	James 1:19-20	What triggers my anger? Why do I get angry? How do I express my anger?
Bondage	Galatians 5:1	What sins am I in bondage to? Why have I held sin against God in my heart? Why do I struggle to be free?

A. Prayer to be used BEFORE each section:

> *"All-Powerful. Almighty, Holy God, I come to You in the name of my Lord Jesus Christ and on His authority. I ask You to remove the enemy from my presence and this room. Oh God, in the mighty name of Jesus, as a child of God, I have been made righteous by the blood of Jesus. I ask You to help me to dismiss all of the enemy's lies that I have been believing and replace them with Your truth. I ask You to go before me and search out my heart, Please soften my heart to humbly acknowledge my sin. I ask the Holy Spirit to convict my heart that I will see my sin as evil and wicked. I declare myself to be Your child in Christ Jesus and I need His power to be free from the bondage of my sin. I surrender this time to You. By the authority and name of Jesus Christ my Lord, I pray, Amen."*

B. Prayer to be used AFTER each section:

> *"In the name of Jesus Christ my Lord and on His authority alone, I declare that every enemy of God release their stronghold on me, that I may be free from bondage to the sin of _____ _____ (name the sin). Oh God, I cry out to You for the evil that I have done before You. I ask for Your gracious forgiveness for the sin of_____ (name the sin) I committed against You. I declare that my Holy God in the name of Jesus has all the power to free me and declare me completely FREE. I praise You in the name of His mighty Son, Jesus Christ, who gives me victory. God, You say in John 8:36, "So if the Son sets you free, you will be free indeed." I hold onto that as truth right now. Thank You, Father. I pray all of this in the name and authority of the Lord Jesus Christ, Amen."*

9. Confession

As a Christian, you have the capacity to walk before God with a clear conscience:

- Confess and forsake known sin. Examine your guilt feelings in light of Scripture. Deal with the sin God's Word reveals (Pr. 28:13; 1 Jn. 1:9; Jas. 5:16; Ps. 32:5).
- Ask forgiveness and be reconciled to anyone you have wronged (Mt. 5:23-24; 6:14-15).
- Make restitution to those you've wronged (Num. 5:6-7; Lk. 19:8; Phil. 19).

- ◆ Don't procrastinate in clearing your wounded conscience.
- ◆ Some people put off dealing with their guilt, thinking their conscience will clear itself in time. It won't. Procrastination allows the guilt feelings to fester. That in turn generates depression, anxiety, and other emotional problems (Ac. 24:16). 5. Educate your conscience. A weak, easily grieved conscience results from a lack of spiritual knowledge (1 Cor. 8:7).[29]

Confessing to God is the first step, but then we must go to the people we have sinned against and confess our sins to them as well. We must seek their forgiveness!

> Most of us have had sins that we would easily confess to God, yet would be ashamed to confess to another brother or sister. Does this make sense? After all, God is the Holy One. To be exposed in His presence should be much more difficult than being exposed before sinners like ourselves. People who truly confess to God are less concerned that others learn their secret. If we easily confess to God something that shames us to confess to a friend, we are thinking too highly of the opinions of people and not highly enough about the holiness of God.[30]
>
> A man who confesses his sins in the presence of a brother knows that he is no longer alone with himself; he experiences the presence of God in the reality of the other person. As long as I am by myself in the confession of my sins, everything remains in the clear, but in the presence of a brother, the sin has to be brought into the light.[31]

10. Forgiveness

Remember all of the people whose names you put stars by? In your notebook, write a list of those names and the offenses associated with each.

Use the guided prayers below to pray over each name, asking God to give you the power to forgive and ask for forgiveness for the sin they committed against you or the sin you have committed against them.

> *"Father God, in the name of Jesus, I choose to forgive*
> *_____ (name) for the hurt, pain, and*
> *rejection I have felt by their actions toward me. I forgive them in*
> *the name of Jesus and ask You to heal the emotional pain I have*
> *experienced. I choose to not believe any lies that may be*

*associated with this action. I now choose to forgive
_____ (named) and surrender them
to You. I lay the sin of my bitterness at Your feet and I declare that
in the power of Jesus's name, I am no longer a slave to this sin,
person, action, or lie. I am free in Christ to live victoriously over
the past and move forward in the power of Jesus's name.
In the mighty name of Jesus, Amen"*

*"Oh Father, I come in the name of Jesus Christ.
My humble heart is sad knowing that I have sinned against my holy
Father. You are deserving of all praise and glory. I ask You to
please forgive me for the sin I have held against
_____ (name). Will You forgive me for the sin
of _____ (sin) I committed against this person and You?
Will You give me the power to contact this person and ask them for
forgiveness? I pray these things in the mighty, all-powerful name of
Jesus, Amen."*

The proper way to ask for forgiveness:

- Contact the person. *
- Acknowledge your sin.
- Accept full responsibility for what you have done.
- Ask their forgiveness, naming the sin.
- Accept their forgiveness with a grateful heart.
- Make any restitution that may be necessary.
- If they are willing to pray with you, seal the deal with a prayer.

*I don't recommend contacting someone from your past that may stir up conflict in your present relationships, or a person who is unstable or dangerous. Simply take their offense or your offense to the Lord privately.

11. Proclaim

Once you are completely done with each section, proclaim your freedom in Christ over these sins using these verses to guide you.

"I have been crucified with Christ. It is no longer I who live, but Christ who lives in me. And the life I now live in the flesh I live by faith in the Son of God, who loved me and gave himself for me" (Galatians 2:20).

"But now that you have been set free from sin and have become slaves of God, the fruit you get leads to sanctification and its end, eternal life" (Romans 6:22).

12. Prayer of Victory

Reread Romans 6 aloud and declare that you are no longer a slave to lies, fear, idols, or bitterness.

In your notebook, write a prayer of thanksgiving to the Lord for setting you free and declaring you free from lies, fear, idols, bitterness, anger, and bondage.

13. Worship

Spend time praising the Lord by reading Psalm 139.

14. My Prayer for You

This is my prayer for you as you leave this Personal Sabbatical:

> "I pray God to fill you with the knowledge of His will in all spiritual wisdom and understanding, so as to walk in a manner worthy of the Lord, fully pleasing to Him: bearing fruit in every good work and increasing in the knowledge of God; being strengthened with all power, according to His glorious might, for all endurance and patience with joy; giving thanks to the Father, who has qualified you to share in the inheritance of the saints in light" Colossians 1:9–12.

15. Closing

The goal of this sabbatical is to help you seek God and allow Him to reveal any sins that have taken up root in your heat. My prayer is that you did find total freedom in the power of Christ today, to live free from the slavery of habitual sins.

But maybe today, during your sabbatical, you didn't feel as though you reached that goal and feel a little defeated or frustrated. I want you to know that I am so thankful you set aside time to allow God to dig into your heart. I know some of those areas were painful to walk through, but you did it. Praise the Lord. I rejoice with you! God is at work in your heart, and it may take a little more time to work through those deep-rooted areas.

Today was a huge step in your sanctifying journey, and remember, it is a journey. God is always at work and will continue to walk you to freedom over the power of sin in your life. That is sanctification. He desires to set you free over the power of sin. Be patient, stay close to God, stay focused on His truth, and rely on the power of the Holy Spirit to push you through to victory.

We all need one another to walk this life together. We were never meant to do it alone. I would highly recommend you find an ACBC-certified counselor in your area to come alongside of you for further guidance.

Certified Biblical Counselors - https://biblicalcounseling.com/counselors/

I pray you will continue to take sabbaticals for the rest of your life. It's a great way to regroup, reevaluate, and take inventory on your relationship with the Lord and allow God to dig deep into your heart. Praise the Lord for His grace and all of the powerful work of Jesus Christ.

EPILOGUE

At the beginning of this book, I said we should try to imagine us sitting across from each other, sipping coffee, me in my front row seat, you across from me, walking this journey together. I was thinking about you as I typed every word in this book. You were the face I imagined as I passionately sought the Lord on what He wanted me to write. I wanted you to be inspired by the power of God's Word and His truth. God's words are premium, life-changing, and redemptive. God's Word is alive and powerful. It is completely centered on the Gospel and the beautiful victory we have because of Jesus Christ our Lord.

The one thing I pray you gained from this book is to treasure your Lord and His words. Like Mary, I pray you choose to value the words of Jesus and make them the one necessary thing in your life. Like Mary, I pray you choose to sit quietly at His feet and let Him speak to your heart in a soft and gentle way. Like Mary, I pray you choose the good portion, Jesus!

"But one thing is necessary. Mary has chosen the good portion, which will not be taken away from her" (Luke 10:42).

I know going through this book was tough for many of you. It's hard to dig into past hurts and heartaches that stir up lots of pain, guilt, and shame. Nobody enjoys that. But you decided your relationship with God was worth it. You chose to surrender those stubborn areas of your heart that you have held onto and been trapped by for so long. Your obedient choices are a testimony of the power of God through Christ in you.

We took quite a journey together, you and I. We walked through, our identity in Christ, the lies we believe, anger and fears, the idols we worship. We walked through the bitterness caused by an unforgiving heart, the cycle of habitual sins that kept us in bondage. With tears, we faced the heartache from the many hurts, discouragements, rejections.

Like you, I have walked through many of the same things. God is in the process of writing my story. He used this book to remind me of His goodness in my own life. I am humbled by His incredibly generous gifts of grace and mercy that He has bestowed upon me throughout my journey with Him. Like you, I am growing and learning every day. He has taken me through some growing seasons that left me crying out for His mercy. There were times of great exhaustion that brought me to my knees in utter discouragement. Times of stubbornness that led me to fight against change and push away from dealing with the root issues of my sinful heart.

Those seasons were tough, but I wouldn't trade them for anything because those hard seasons were some of the most precious memories. I can remember sitting in my closet, my personal quiet sanctuary, and literally crying my eyes out to God. I needed God and was desperate to draw close to Him. I believed this verse: "Let us then with confidence draw near to the throne of grace, that we may receive mercy and find grace to help in time of need" (Hebrews 4:16).

I needed His mercy. I felt the circumstances of the moment were more than I could bear. But what makes those times so treasured in my mind is the incredible sense of God's presence amid all my tears. He was there to scoop me up and hold me through those incredibly hard times when I didn't think I could go on.

Spending time with God and poring over His words refreshed my soul and brought joy to my heart. Like David I learned that the commands of the Lord are radiant and the fear of the Lord pure, firm, and righteous. Spending time with God and reading His word brought me great joy.

"The law of the Lord is perfect, refreshing the soul. The statutes of the Lord are trustworthy, making wise the simple. The precepts of the Lord are right, giving joy to the heart. The commands of the Lord are radiant, giving light to the eyes. The fear of the Lord is pure, enduring forever. The decrees of the Lord are firm, and all of them are righteous" (Psalm 19:7–9).

As God continues to write my story, I pray that my heart will always be knitted close to His, my eyes will be enlightened to His truth, and that I will say I believe the commands of the Lord are radiant and He is pure and enduring forever.

God is writing your life story, a beautiful love story, that is unique and magnificent. He has a glorious story to write that includes, joy, contentment, peace, growth, and restoration. He has created you to reflect the image of His Son Jesus. He promises to be faithful, steadfast, and forgiving every single day of your life. He will never leave you nor forsake you. "It is the Lord who goes before you. He will be with you; he will not leave you or forsake you. Do not fear or be dismayed" (Deuteronomy 31:8).

I encourage you to continue to value the things God values, treasure God and His Word, secure them deep into your soul, and meditate on them day and night. Reflect the Good News of Jesus Christ to your family, your neighbors, your community and wherever God takes you in this life.

Don't ever give up fighting, striving, or yearning for truth. Stay close to God, stay in His Word, and tell others about Jesus. Wake up every day and thank God for the day He has given you. Rejoice! Praise! Choose joy!! And when you sin, repent quickly, ask for forgiveness immediately, and lay it at the feet of Jesus and worship.

The one most necessary thing … choose the Good Portion!
*"My flesh and my heart may fail, but God is the strength of my heart and my **portion** forever"*
(Psalm 73:26).

*"The Lord is my **portion**," says my soul, "therefore I will hope in Him"*
(Lamentations 3:24).

*"The Lord is my **portion**; I promise to keep your word"*
(Psalm 119:57).

*"The Lord is my chosen **portion** and my cup; you hold my lot"*
(Psalm 16:5).

*My Prayer for you ... that you will always intentionally choose the Good **Portion**!*

My prayer is that you will always and intentionally do as Mary did in Luke 10. Mary, who sat at the Lord's feet and listened to his teaching, did the one thing that was necessary. Mary has chosen the Good Portion, which will not be taken away from her.

Closing Prayer:

"For this reason, I kneel before the Father, from whom his whole family in heaven and on earth derives its name. I pray that out of his glorious riches he may strengthen you with power through his Spirit in your inner being, so that Christ may dwell in your hearts through faith. And I pray that you, being rooted and established in love, may have power, together with all the saints, to grasp how wide and long and high and deep is the love of Christ, and to know this love that surpasses knowledge—that you may be filled to the measure of all the fullness of God. Now to him who is able to do immeasurably more than all we ask or imagine, according to his power that is at work within us, to him be glory in the church and in Christ Jesus throughout all generations, forever and ever!" Amen. (Ephesians 3:14–21)

To God be the Glory!

Love you my sweet sisters,
Heidi

The Good Portion - 30-Day Devotional

I know you are ready and eager to continue spending treasured time with your Heavenly Father. I'm so grateful for your choice to do so.

Jesus commends Mary for "choosing the one thing necessary, the good portion." The decision to value Jesus and His Word is a priceless choice we must all make. You are choosing the one good thing, to value and treasure your relationship with Him. Praise the Lord.

The Good Portion —30-day Devotional is a useful tool to guide you further in your intentional pursuit of God and His truth. I've creatively arranged this devotional to lead you into a deeper, more intimate walk with Him and the knowledge of His word.

The chart below is a guide to help you learn to create a good habit of setting aside personal time each day to be still, quiet and worshipful before your Heavenly Father.

My prayer for you as you continue to choose the "Good Portion" and spend time investing in eternal things:

"I pray that out of His glorious riches He may strengthen you with power through His Spirit in your inner being, so that Christ may dwell in your hearts through faith. And I pray that you, being rooted and established in love, may have power, together with all the Lord's holy people, to grasp how wide and long and high and deep is the love of Christ, and to know this love that surpasses knowledge—that you may be filled to the measure of all the fullness of God" (Ephesians 3:16-19).

30 Day Devotional Daily Guide

What you'll need - Bible, an empty journal or notebook, pen.
Time commitment - One uninterrupted hour per day.
Use this guide to help walk you through your quiet time each day.

Open in Prayer	A. Start by thanking God for the privilege to spend intimate time with Him. B. Thank Him for allowing you the opportunity to come into His presence. C. Ask God to give you a teachable spirit and open your eyes to His truth.
Scripture Reading	Read the daily selected Psalm.
Journal	Write down key truths, that stood out to you, using the daily selected Psalm.
Confession	Acknowledge and write down any unconfessed sins. Repent and ask God for His gracious forgiveness. (I John 1:9)
Supplication	Write down your prayer requests, date them and commit them to God. Once God gives you a definitive answer, write out the results and date it.
Gratitude	Give thanks for an attribute of God using the attribute listed for that day.
Worship	Use the daily Psalm as a guide to help you worship and praise God.
Daily Meditation	Meditate on the daily verse. Hiding God's Word in your heart is so important.

Day 1	
Attribute of God	Holy
Scripture Reading	Psalm 99
Daily Meditation	Vs. 9 - "Exalt the Lord our God and worship at his holy mountain; for the Lord our God is holy!"

Day 2	
Attribute of God	Glory
Scripture Reading	Psalm 96
Daily Meditation	Vs. 3 - "Declare his glory among the nations, his marvelous works among all the peoples!"

Day 3	
Attribute of God	Faithful
Scripture Reading	Psalm 111
Daily Meditation	Vs. 7 - "The works of His hands are faithful and just; all His precepts are trustworthy."

Day 4	
Attribute of God	Love
Scripture Reading	Psalm 136
Daily Meditation	Vs. 1, 2 - "Give thanks to the Lord, for He is good, for His steadfast love endures forever. Give thanks to the God of gods, for His steadfast love endures forever."

Day 5	
Attribute of God	Creator
Scripture Reading	Psalm 104
Daily Meditation	Vs. 24 "O Lord, how manifold are Your works. In wisdom have You made them all; the earth is full of Your creatures."

Day 6	
Attribute of God	Protector
Scripture Reading	Psalm 91
Daily Meditation	Vs. 2 - "I will say to the Lord, 'My Refuge and my Fortress, my God, in Whom I trust.'"

Day 7	
Attribute of God	Shepherd
Scripture Reading	Psalm 23
Daily Meditation	Vs.1,2 - "The Lord is my shepherd; I shall not want. He makes me lie down in green pastures, He leads me beside still waters. He restores my soul..He leads me in paths of righteousness for his name's sake."

Day 8	
Attribute of God	Teacher
Scripture Reading	Psalm 25
Daily Meditation	vs. 9 - "He leads the humble in what is right, and teaches the humble His way."

Day 9	
Attribute of God	Grace
Scripture Reading	Psalm 86
Daily Meditation	Vs.15 - "But you, O Lord, are a God merciful and gracious, slow to anger and abounding in steadfast love and faithfulness."

Day 10	
Attribute of God	Majestic
Scripture Reading	Psalm 45
Daily Meditation	Vs. 4 - "In your majesty ride out victoriously for the cause of truth and meekness and righteousness; let your right hand teach you awesome deeds!"

Day 11	
Attribute of God	Keeper
Scripture Reading	Psalm 121
Daily Meditation	Vs. 8 - "The Lord will keep your going out and your coming in from this time forth and forevermore."

Day 12	
Attribute of God	Refuge
Scripture Reading	Psalm 142
Daily Meditation	Vs.5 - "I cry to you, O Lord; I say, "You are my refuge, my portion in the land of the living."

Day 13	
Attribute of God	Good
Scripture Reading	Psalm 118
Daily Meditation	Vs. 1 - "Oh give thanks to the Lord, for He is Good; for His steadfast love endures forever!"

Day 14	
Attribute of God	Great
Scripture Reading	Psalm 145
Daily Meditation	Vs. 3 - "Great is the Lord, and greatly to be praised, and His greatness is unsearchable."

Day 15	
Attribute of God	Fortress
Scripture Reading	Psalm 46
Daily Meditation	Vs. 11 - "The Lord of hosts is with us; the God of Jacob is our fortress."

Day 16	
Attribute of God	Omnipotent
Scripture Reading	Psalm 147
Daily Meditation	Vs. 5 - "Great is our Lord, and abundant in power; His understanding is beyond measure."

Day 17	
Attribute of God	King
Scripture Reading	Psalm 24
Daily Meditation	Vs. 10 - "Who is this King of glory? The Lord of hosts, He is the King of glory! Selah."

Day 18	
Attribute of God	Omnicient
Scripture Reading	Psalm 139
Daily Meditation	Vs. 1, 2 - "O Lord, You have searched me and known me! You know when I sit down and when I rise up, You discern my thoughts from afar."

Day 19	
Attribute of God	Immutable
Scripture Reading	Psalm 41
Daily Meditation	Vs. 13 - "Blessed be the Lord, the God of Israel, from everlasting to everlasting! Amen and Amen."

Day 20	
Attribute of God	Trustworthy
Scripture Reading	Psalm 56
Daily Meditation	Vs. 10, 11 - "In God, whose word I praise, in the Lord, whose word I praise, in God I trust; I shall not be afraid. What can man do to me?"

Day 21	
Attribute of God	Perfect
Scripture Reading	Psalm 18
Daily Meditation	Vs. 30 - "This God—His way is perfect; the Word of the Lord proves true; He is a shield for all those who take refuge in Him."

Day 22	
Attribute of God	Lord
Scripture Reading	Psalm 100
Daily Meditation	Vs. 3 - "Know that the Lord, He is God. It is He who made us, and we are His, we are His people, and the sheep of His pasture."

Day 23	
Attribute of God	Eternal
Scripture Reading	Psalm 48
Daily Meditation	Vs. 14 - "That this is God, our God forever and ever. He will guide us forever."

Day 24	
Attribute of God	Steadfast
Scripture Reading	Psalm 102
Daily Meditation	Vs. 12 - "But you, O Lord, are enthroned forever; You are remembered throughout all generations."

Day 25	
Attribute of God	Deliverer
Scripture Reading	Psalm 37
Daily Meditation	Vs. 40 - "The Lord helps them and delivers them; He delivers them from the wicked and saves them because they take refuge in Him."

Day 26	
Attribute of God	Sustainer
Scripture Reading	Psalm 55
Daily Meditation	Vs. 22 - "Cast your burden on the Lord, and He will sustain you. He will never permit the righteous to be moved."

Day 27	
Attribute of God	Mercy
Scripture Reading	Psalm 103
Daily Meditation	Vs. 8 - "The Lord is merciful and gracious, slow to anger and abounding in steadfast love."

Day 28	
Attribute of God	Righteous
Scripture Reading	Psalm 36
Daily Meditation	Vs. 10 - "Oh, continue Your steadfast love to those who know You, and Your righteousness to the upright of heart!"

Day 29	
Attribute of God	Strong Tower
Scripture Reading	Psalm 61
Daily Meditation	Vs. 2b, 3 - "Lead me to the rock that is higher than I, for you have been my refuge, a strong tower against the enemy."

Day 30	
Attribute of God	Savior
Scripture Reading	Psalm 65
Daily Meditation	Vs. 5 - "By awesome deeds You answer us with righteousness, O God of our salvation."

Acknowledgements

Nothing I have done in this life have I accomplished on my own. Not one single thing. From birth, till God takes me home, I cannot take credit for one personal achievement that someone wasn't there to guide me, direct me, uplift me, encourage me or provide for me. God has graciously and undeservedly given me the gift of salvation through my Lord and Savior, Jesus Christ. That is the greatest gift I have ever received. There is nothing worth living for or accomplishing in this life without it being done for the Glory of God in honor of His Son Jesus.

God's graciousness and mercy for me did not end at the cross. He continues to lavish me with a lifetime of amazing generous blessings every day. 38 years ago, God knew this young, naive 20-year-old girl would need a strong, wise, kind, gentle, sweet man to take care of her. God truly gave me the best. Many times I just sit, lost in thought, and wonder how I was chosen to be this man's wife. How? How have I been so blessed? I am incredibly grateful to have my sweet husband, Mike Baird, my best friend, and adventurous partner to do this life with. He has inspired me to dig deep into God's word, to be a good Berean of scripture and to interpret the truth correctly. His love for reading, history and learning has inspired and influenced our entire family to seek out God's truth with passion. You will see much of my husband's influence throughout this book.

Mike, you have been my greatest cheerleader, supporter, defender and prayer warrior throughout this book-writing journey. You have been by my side, encouraging me to keep going, when I wasn't sure I should or could. You kept me on track when I wanted to stray. Your kind words and gentle nudges have been exactly what I needed to make it though. And what would I do without all your logistical and technical support as well? Thank you for taking care of all these areas outside my wheelhouse. My hero, my love and my bestie, I adore you. Thank you, sweet man.

Michael (our oldest) and Jamie… you two inspire me with perseverance and faithfulness. Watching you with our three precious granddaughters, Hadley, Willa, and Ellis has inspired me. You are such loving, kind and patient parents. Jamie, do you remember the day you brought the girls over for a quick visit, Hadley (5 yr. old) walked right through the front door, handed me a much needed cold ice tea, and said, with a huge thumbs up, "Good job on the book writing, Nana." It's times like these that you all spurred me to keep going. Thanks for your patience as I went awol hiding out writing for weeks.

Zack and Kristen (2nd born)… I am so grateful for the lessons you two have taught me on joy. No matter the circumstance, you choose to be joyful. Watching you two support each other through years of infertility and miscarriages has been truly remarkable. Your heart for ministry and hospitality is priceless. Kristen, I had no idea how much time, effort and prayer went into writing a book. Watching you become a published author gave me the vision to persevere even when I was unsure, tired or losing hope. Your words of encouragement went a long way. Thank you!

Dav and Bethany(3rd born)…what a fun year watching you two get married and now live life as adorable newlyweds. You both have such a heart for ministry and others. You wasted no time as a married couple jumping in and serving the body of Christ as a team. You are true examples of living life with excitement, enthusiasm, and intentionality. Thank you for giving me the vision to write a book when I said over and over, "No. You and Kristen write books, I could never do that." Thank you for setting the example to be faithful, steadfast and trust in God's timing.

Stephen, (4th born)… you and I are alike in so many ways. We are both passionate, expressive, emotional, and we speak a million words a day, each! I am always enlightened as you openly share your heart so transparently, giving me thoughtful pause to do the same. No one can tell a story with more expression and enthusiasm than you. Many of the words in this book were inspired by you. Thank you for helping me see life from a different perspective and through different lenses.

Ellissa, (5th born)… girl, what a sweetheart. I have learned a lot from watching you serve others with Christ-like hospitality and selflessness. Opening our home to give others a place to feel loved and blessed is one of the many ways you reflect God's character so beautifully. Then you decided to go halfway around the world to take care of precious orphans in China, a vision you had since you were a little girl. Watching you create and teach a class using your experiences and pushing outside your comfort zone, is what has inspired me to do so many things, including writing this book. Thank you!

Timothy (6th born)… talk about a guy that has a little bit of amazingness in all areas of life. You have always lived your life with such an intentional purpose and plan. You see things with such a curious and creative eye. I want to live life through your eyes just for a day. I marvel at your adventurous spirit to try something new and exciting. You live outside the box, but always giving glory to God for everything. Thanks for motivating me to be adventurous and more creative.

Rebekah (7th born)…God knew this family would need a truly skilled manager to help us all in this busy season of our lives. God raised you up to fill the managerial role in the family business as well as in Girl Defined Ministries. Where would we all be without our Beks? Seriously! We are so blessed by your sweet, kind attitude and heart to serve others. Your incredible work ethics and desire to do everything with godly excellence has influenced me to do the same as I wrote this book. Thank you!

Suzanna (8th born)… Sue, you really got me through this book writing every single day. We sat for hours typing away on our computers, you doing school and me writing this book. Day after day, hour after hour… it was your sweet spontaneous hugs throughout the day that brought such encouragement right when I needed it. Annnddd… A HUGE thank you for partnering with me by designing the cover and all the inside artwork of this book. God has gifted you with amazing art skills that have blessed thousands of people around the world. P

Matthew (9th born)… Although you were only with us for such a short time, God used you to change our hearts forever. We have never been the same. Each of us look at life through different lenses, we are more sensitive to the brevity of life and find ourselves making the most of every moment. We still celebrate your precious life every year as a family, taking the time to give God the Glory. Whether we live a day or 99 years, life is precious at conception and we praise God for every moment of life. We miss you and long for the day we will see you again in heaven. Your sweet story is forever written in the pages of this book.

Thank you to my sweet parents, Mitchell and Helga Mick… I love our morning coffee chats over Skype and thank you for always asking me how I was doing with the book. I appreciate your wise counsel as I bounced ideas and thoughts off of you and for your faithful prayers for me every day. You're the best. I love you both.

To all my dear family and friends who faithfully prayed and encouraged me throughout this process, I felt those prayers and all your sweet words that came just when I needed them. All that I wrote in this book, came from what I have been so privileged to learn from so many others like you. To God be the Glory for His Son Jesus Christ, my Lord!

I love you all…

[1] John Piper Reference: God's Passion for His Glory, p. 41. Crossway Books; 59281st edition (January 6, 2006)

[2] Edward T. Welch, When People are Big and God is Small Series: Resources for Changing Lives / Paperback: 256 pages / Publisher: P & R Publishing; 32132nd edition (June 1, 1997) ©1997

[3] C.H. Spurgeon Reference: Morning and Evening, Morning May 16. Crossway Books; Revised, Updated edition (September 26, 2003)

[4] Desiring God, PO Box 2901 Minneapolis, Minnesota 55402, USA © The Desiring God Foundation 2009 Paperback, 208 pages Published March 20, 2009 by Christian Focus Publications (first published January 1st 2009)

[5] Redeemer Presbyterian Church Resources / Gospel in Life. Sermon: "Peace-Overcoming Anxiety" By Tim Keller https://www.brightontheday.com/sermon-peace-overcoming-anxiety-by-tim-keller/ February 18, 1990 Podcast series

[6] Counterfeit Gods: The Empty Promises of Money, Sex, and Power, and the Only Hope that Matters Paperback by Timothy Keller (Author) Publisher: Penguin Books; Reprint edition (October 4, 2011)

[7] Reference: Edward Welch Reference: Addictions – A Banquet in the Grave, P&R Publishing, 2001, p. 198 gracequotes.org/topic/sin-confession / P&R Publishing, 2001, p. 49, Used by Permission.

[8] Reference: Edward Welch Reference: Addictions – A Banquet in the Grave, P&R Publishing, 2001, p. 198 gracequotes.org/topic/sin-confession / P&R Publishing, 2001, p. 49, Used by Permission.

[9] David Powlison, "Idols of the Heart and 'Vanity Fair'," Christian Counseling & Educational Foundation (CCEF) Online: http://www.ccef.org/idols-heart-and-vanity-fair (October 16, 2009).

[10] Elise Fitzpatrick © 2001 Idols of the Heart / P & R Publishing Company PO Box 817 Philipsburg, New Jersey 08865

[11] Ed Welch, Side by Side: Walking with Others in Wisdom and Love goodreads.com/work/quotes/42780899-side-by-side-walking-with-others-in-wisdom-and-love.

[12] What-is-sanctification-for-christians#_edn1 Blog/ What is Sanctification For Christians? by Guest Writer on May 04, 2016 Jellytelly.com/blog/

[13] John Piper - FEBRUARY 11, 2007 Resource by John Piper: *Sermon / Marriage: God's Showcase of Covenant-Keeping Grace*

[14] John Piper - FEBRUARY 11, 2007 Resource by John Piper: Sermon / Marriage: God's Showcase of Covenant-Keeping Grace

[15] John MacArthur / Reference: Total Forgiveness and the Confession of Sin, The article originally appeared (http://www.gty.org/resources/sermons/62-8) at www.gty.org. © 1969-2008. Grace to You. All Rights Reserved.

[16] Neil T. Anderson - The Steps to Freedom in Christ © 1990, 2001, 2004, 2017 Publisher: Bethany House Publishers 11400 Hampshire Avenue South / Bloomington, Minnesota 55438 Baker Publishing Company / Grand Rapids, Michigan

[17] Resolving Conflict: How to Make, Disturb and Keep Peace, Phillipsburg, N.J.: Presbyterian and Reformed Publishing, © 2014 by Louis Paul Priolo.

[18] Resolving Conflict: How to Make, Disturb and Keep Peace, Phillipsburg, N.J.: Presbyterian and Reformed Publishing, © 2014 by Louis Paul Priolo.

[19] John Piper - Why Can't I Overcome My Bitterness and Anger? MAY 26, 2008 www.desiringgod.org/interviews/why-cant-i-overcome-my-bitterness-and-anger

[20] Resolving Conflict: How to Make, Disturb and Keep Peace, Phillipsburg, N.J.: Presbyterian and Reformed Publishing, © 2014 by Louis Paul Priolo.

[21] Resolving Conflict: How to Make, Disturb and Keep Peace, Phillipsburg, N.J.: Presbyterian and Reformed Publishing, © 2014 by Louis Paul Priolo.

[22] John MacArthur - Reference: Is There Ever a Just Reason for It? The sermon originally appeared (www.gty.org/library/sermons-library/42-44/true-repentance-gods-highway-to-the-heart-part-4) at www.gty.org. © 1969-2008. Grace to You.

[23] Goodreads.com/work/quotes/42780899-side-by-side-walking-with-others-in-wisdom-and-love

[24] What-is-sanctification-for-christians#_edn1 Blog/ What is Sanctification For Christians? by Guest Writer on May 04, 2016 jellytelly.com/blog

[25] Edward Welch Reference: Blame it on the Brain?, p. 197. Publisher: P & R Publishing (June 1, 1998)

[26] Edward Welch - Reference: Addictions – A Banquet in the Grave, P&R Publishing, 2001, p. 54-55

[27] What-is-sanctification-for-christians#_edn1 Blog/ What is Sanctification For Christians? by Guest Writer on May 04, 2016 jellytelly.com/blog

[28] What-is-sanctification-for-christians#_edn1 Blog/ What is Sanctification For Christians? by Guest Writer on May 04, 2016 jellytelly.com/blog

[29] Reference: Adapted from: Keeping a Pure Conscience, The article originally appeared (www.gty.org/Resources/Articles/23) at www.gty.org. © 1969-2008. Grace to You.

[30] Edward Welch Reference: Addictions – A Banquet in the Grave, P&R Publishing, 2001, p. 198 gracequotes.org/topic/sin-confession/

[31] Dietrich Bonhoeffer Reference: Life Together, Harper and Row, 1954, p. 20. gracequotes.org/topic/sin-confession

Contact Heidi Baird
for
Speaking
Engagements
and
Events

Instagram - @heidimbaird

Facebook - @heidimbaird

Email - hbaird@abiz4me.com

Made in the USA
Middletown, DE
22 December 2020